Growing Food in Solar Greenhouses

*A Month–by–Month Guide to
Raising Vegetables, Fruit
and Herbs Under Glass*

A Sun Words Book

Dolphin Books
Doubleday & Company, Inc.
Garden City, New York

Growing Food in Solar Greenhouses

*A Month–by–Month Guide to
Raising Vegetables, Fruit and Herbs Under Glass*

By Delores Wolfe

832

Illustrated by Richards Steinbock   Foreword by Susan Yanda

A Sun Words Book

Dolphin Books

Doubleday & Company, Inc.

ISBN 0-385-17602-3

Library of Congress Catalog card number 81-43243

Copyright © 1981 by Delores Wolfe

First Edition

Designed by Michael Havey

ACKNOWLEDGMENTS

*I*n any work of this nature, the information found in it is derived from many sources in addition to the experiences of the author. Those contributing in very meaningful ways must be given credit because, without them, this book would not be complete.

June Fuerderer, friend and fellow greenhouse grower, first started me thinking about growing fruit under glass. Bud Winsor, a commercial grower, and instructor in the Department of Horticulture at the Cheshire County Vocational Center, brought theory into the realm of the practical. Bud and June both assisted me on the Resources chapter. Charles Scheaff, local raiser of dwarf rabbits, took the time to explain why rabbits do not belong in greenhouses.

People knowledgeable in the art of growing food under glass in various sections of the country read the manuscript and offered many helpful comments. The emphasis they placed on the regional character-istics of solar greenhouse gardens led to the garden types defined in the book. My gratitude for this labor goes to Sara Balcomb (Southwest), Susan Yanda (Southwest and Southeast), Abby Marier (North Central) and Loretta Powell (Mid-Atlantic). Janis Kobran copy-read the manuscript to make sure I did not leave too many questions unanswered.

Many thanks go to Susan Yanda who took time out from a busy schedule to write the foreword for this book.

Behind every author stands an editor—the unsung hero of the written word—who, in addition to correcting language and spelling, serves as a sound-ing board, offers suggestions and criticisms that result in a better book, and calms shattered nerves as the deadline approaches. Sandra Oddo of Sun Words filled that capacity and more. Working with her has been a major learning experience that made writing this book more fun than chore. In her role as ama-teur gardener *cum* future solar greenhouse grower, she asked perceptive questions and demanded practical explanations. Her faith in the need for this book was important and contributed to its completion.

Richard Steinbock's drawings and Michael Havey's book design do much to endow the words contained herein with a vitality of their own.

My family deserves more thanks than I can ever give them. Our children started us off on the road to farming and alternatives in living, and have kept that interest very much alive. My husband, Fred, gave me the time and space to do my writing. He read manu-scripts, made useful comments, and kept life going while I took time out from other obligations to com-plete it. His support during the past year has been great and very necessary to a fledgling author. And finally to my parents who first gave me the room to grow and to Fred and our children who made sure I continued the process, the bond of love and apprecia-tion has been deepened by this experience.

*T*his morning as I read the newspaper, two articles caught my eye. One headline read "Oil Decontrol Pinches Consumers" and a very graphic chart showed how in the last five years home heating oil has almost tripled in price and regular gasoline has more than tripled. The other headline, much more frightening, read "Empty Bellies Are Reason For Hunger Week." The empty bellies are not just in Third World or developing nations, but are also here in the United States where an estimated 12 million people dwell in a kind of poverty that leaves the stomach empty each night; where many, especially the elderly and people on fixed incomes, must choose between heating and eating. Not in today's paper, but probably in tomorrow's will be more about the shortage of water in New England, the lack of snow cover in the Rockies, which portends drought conditions for the coming summer. We think about these water problems because they make the daily news and affect our winter skiing. I have yet to read a headline in the daily news that warns us that we are using up our ground water. We rarely read of the erosion robbing tons of topsoil annually.

It is fairly recently that as a nation we have begun to look at the environment, the closed system of the earth that we inhabit. It is frightening, really, to look at these problems because there are not many ready answers to what we will do to provide solutions. There is a fear of great life style changes, of deprivation of things that have become a large part of our way of life. There is little feeling that by becoming guardians of our ecosystem, our lives will be enhanced rather than depleted. Enter the solar greenhouse.

The term, solar greenhouse, means different things to different people. For many it is a heat producing addition; for others it is a warm, sunny living space; for still others it is the joy of a year–round garden. Though I have enjoyed many a happy hour luxuriating in the warmth of a solar greenhouse, true benefits of the greenhouse for me come from the gardening, the production of fresh, delicious vegetables year–round, vegetables aplenty to feed both family and friends. There is the winter greenhouse, when it is well below freezing outside, the days are cold and raw and I can be amid petunias and fig trees, tending the greenhouse and picking the fresh vegetables we will eat that day. It is a time away from the whirlwind hurriedness that seems to be so much a part of the day, a time spent watching a small piece of nature evolve in its quiet and systematic way. There is the summer greenhouse, where I also spend a lot of time, although I am an avid outdoor gardener. There is not, of course, the extreme temperature difference between the inside and out that is found during the wintertime, nor is there the feeling of warm verdant growth when outside it is cold and barren, but rather there is the predictability of the summer greenhouse garden. I do not worry about the lack of rain, small rabbits, raccoons or skunks, or ravaging hailstorms.

The solar greenhouse garden is a small microcosm of nature, where the greenhouse gardener is the guardian. As the outdoor gardener works with nature, so must the greenhouse gardener become attuned to the systems and rhythms of his or her own particular greenhouse. By doing this, the greenhouse gardener creates an environment that grows and evolves with a life force of its own. What is important is to learn, understand, and work with that force. When you garden in the greenhouse, when you sow the seeds, nurture the soil, water and fertilize the plants, strive to keep the ever-present insect population under control, you begin both to conserve the finite resources that are so rapidly dwindling and to create an environment that brings personal fulfillment.

As you live with your greenhouse, you learn that it has moods, ups and downs, and you begin to react and interact with the system much as you would with a person. There are the joys in the relationship, the fresh produce, the clean air, the time well spent. There are the sorrows, the favorite plant that has become too old and tired to fight off insects and disease and must be discarded, the sudden freeze last night that killed off your budding tomato plant, the fact that you have done everything in your power, and your greenhouse still is not living up to expectations. But overall is the knowledge that you are working toward a self-sustaining future, one in which you have control and by which you have been able to remove yourself to some degree from the mass-dependence age. The energy crisis, the soil crisis, the water crisis, all touch every part of our lives. It is hard to accept personal responsibility for these crises, but as individuals and in our communities we can begin to alleviate some of them. Having a solar greenhouse garden means that you are not at the whim of each rise in oil prices, of each shortage of water, of further use of chemicals necessary to replace the top soil that is no longer there. Having a solar greenhouse garden means that you can to a large extent break the dependence cycle. Having a solar greenhouse garden means that you can plan for next year and the year after that, rather than having your life dictated to you by the morning headlines.

The last ten years have seen exciting growth both in the design and the construction of attached solar greenhouses around the country. But what to do with the greenhouse once it has been built? Only now is information beginning to become available for the greenhouse gardener. I was very excited to hear that Delores Wolfe was writing a book on greenhouse gardening that would be available nationally. In this book, Delores tells how to set the stage to make your vision of your greenhouse a reality as she writes about the weather, what plants to grow when, seed, seedlings, soil, watering, and pest control. There are a few more points to add which have nothing really to do with the mechanics of greenhouse operation,

but are concerned with things I have learned as I have tended my greenhouse for six years, things I have learned as Bill and I have criss-crossed the country building and teaching about greenhouses.

- Think through carefully what you want your greenhouse to look like and decide how much time you have and are willing to give to bring that picture to fruition. The time you spend is directly proportional to what you will get from your greenhouse.

- Spend time observing. This is a wonderful way to get to know your greenhouse. It is a fascinating lesson in understanding the nature of plant growth and of insect life. You will find that soon you will see things you have never noticed before. You will learn to spot problems before they become serious or of epidemic proportions. You will learn to recognize and understand the life force that makes your greenhouse what it is. This time of observation can be as little as five minutes a day, but you will find nothing that pays off so well. And as you observe, record what you see. Your journal will allow you to compare and your knowledge will begin to accumulate into an understanding of the microcosm you are guarding.

- Plant in the greenhouse only those vegetables you and your family enjoy eating, or wish to grow to expand your taste and nutritional horizons. To do any differently is a waste of your time and greenhouse space.

- Plant in the greenhouse only those vegetables that are not easily grown and stored from the outdoor summer garden. Such vegetables as potatoes, carrots, and winter squash take up valuable space and growing time.

- Before you plant, think about energy-in/energy-out. Growing a crop of tomatoes, cucumbers, or peppers in the dead of winter not only will take a lot of time, but will call for added heat and light. (I do always carry one tomato plant, located against the north wall, through the winter greenhouse, hoping to add about one tomato a week to my winter salad.)

- Plant flowers even if your greenhouse is a vegetable producing unit. Marigolds and nasturtiums help to build up the soil and repel insects, but most important, they and other flowers add beauty to your greenhouse—which means that you will want to spend more time in your greenhouse, which means...(see the first point).

Collect as many seed catalogs from as many varied sources as you can. They are fun to read and are chock full of information on special greenhouse varieties, disease-resistant varieties, dwarf varieties, and new varieties.

Experiment in your greenhouse. Let your imagination run as you think of things to grow and eat. Edible chrysanthemums and nasturtiums add life to a winter salad.

If you have children, invite them to tend the greenhouse with you. Children love to work with plants and there is great joy in watching them make discoveries. I find they often see things I have overlooked. And it is fun, and an easy way to help the child learn order, cause and effect, and love of life.

Trust yourself and your intuition in the greenhouse. There is no such person as "the greenhouse gardener." I am a greenhouse gardener, but I am not a horticulturist. I have met many people who grow wonderful outdoor gardens but are sure they cannot grow a radish in the greenhouse. For them there is a mystique surrounding a person who can grow in a greenhouse. So I tell them of some of the people I have met who are greenhouse gardeners: one whose job took her away for long periods of time; one who could not read or write and who bought seeds by the pictures on the jackets; one who did have a degree in horticulture; one whose life was a shambles in all ways, but who was able to keep it somewhat together because of the greenhouse; one who was a student in elementary school; one who was eighty-two years old and could hardly move for arthritis; one whose greenhouse looked like a storage shed filled with nothing but old cardboard boxes and paint cans until things were shuffled around a bit to uncover incredible growth. All had growing greenhouses of which they were proud. So what is a profile of a greenhouse gardener? It is a person who wants a beautiful, producing space, one who is willing to spend the time to experiment, observe, and learn, one who loves this planet we live on and wants to make a contribution to its lasting care and continuance.

Last, but most important, *enjoy* your greenhouse garden and all of the wonderful benefits that ensue from your time and energy put into it.

Susan Yanda

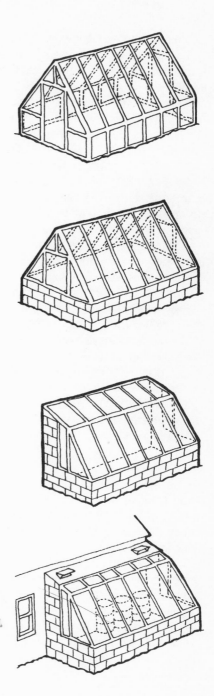

*P*lants need sunlight and warmth. For hundreds of years growers have known that panes of glass—glass houses—inserted between the plant and the sun will let the light in and hold the heat, too, defeating cold seasons or at least shortening them, and lengthening the growing seasons for food and flowers. Hence, greenhouses.

A solar greenhouse is different from a conventional glass house, however, both simpler and more sophisticated. The standard greenhouse consists of single plates of glass laid more or less loosely in frames to form four glass walls. Because glass is not a particularly good insulator, most conventional greenhouses must add heat if plants are to grow in the winter, and the cost of that heat can be substantial. The many known and anonymous designers whose work resulted in the concepts behind solar greenhouse design all began again at the beginning: where's the sun? where's the plant? what's heat and how can you hold onto it?

In all but the southernmost parts of the northern hemisphere, the sun is never overhead. It rides across the southern sky year-round. It is higher in the sky in summer and lower in winter. Why, then, make the north greenhouse wall—where the sun isn't—out of glass? Insulate it, instead. The east and west walls let sunlight in for only fractions of the day, and the fractions are longer in the summer when most greenhouses want to lose, rather than gain, heat. Therefore, make them half-solid and insulate. If there is a roof, make that half-solid, too.

There's still a lot of glass, letting out a lot of heat. Hmmm—how about double layers of glass, carefully sealed? That will hardly hinder the passage of light and will double the barrier to heat escaping. Sunlight can get through glass best if it can hit the glass head-on, at right angles. Therefore, the south glass wall could be tilted to form right angles to incoming winter sunlight when you need heat most. Or it could be placed upright, where the acute angle would cause the most summer sun to be reflected away.

Wait a minute. Does the glazing on a greenhouse have to be *glass*? Well, no. Many rigid plastics and fiberglass products now on the market—and even such inexpensive flexible plastics as polyethylene or bubble-plastic packing material—will let light through just fine. In fact, a lot of plants seem to prefer light that is diffused and bounced around by a plastic glazing, as long as enough gets through to meet growing needs.

That light percentage is critical, because light is the most critical factor to affect plant growth (soil temperature is second). A solar greenhouse has less glazing than a conventional greenhouse, and solid walls in a lot of places. Therefore the solar greenhouse grower must be more sophisticated about such things as microclimates within the greenhouse, and about using every bit of light at hand. Solar greenhouses often have reflective back walls, and pieces of the structure that are not needed for absorbing heat will be painted white. Where heat is intended to soak in, the structure may be painted odd colors—dark reds or blues, for instance, so that heat can be absorbed and the proper light wavelengths maintained at the same time.

So now, instead of a fragile glass house you have a sheltered, tightly sealed growing space that's easy to warm while the sun shines on it. How do you hold that heat for the night? Answer: thermal mass, a great quantity of something heavy—rocks, water and/or soil—that can soak up extra heat during the day, like a sponge, to release it slowly at night when temperatures fall. Suppose, however, that the problem is too much heat in the summer. Solution: vents, large openings low on the front and sides of the greenhouse and high in the roof and at the back, to let outside air pass through to remove unwanted heat and moisture.

Presto: *solar* greenhouse.

A solar greenhouse, therefore, has these qualities:

- The heat necessary to grow plants is supplied by the sun, not by fossil fuel sources. In order to arrange this, the solar greenhouse is designed so that...

- Most of its glazed surfaces face south; all of its glazed surfaces are double-glazed and carefully sealed to keep air from moving around haphazardly.

- Any wall that is not glazed, is insulated. Probably there is movable insulation to cover the glazing and to reduce heat loss at night.

- The greenhouse includes thermal mass to store heat, either in the walls, in the floor, in the beds, or in containers arranged to be in the path of the sun.

- The solar greenhouse is carefully vented, so that the collection and storage of heat is under the control of the greenhouse keeper, not entirely at the whim of sun and weather.

A solar greenhouse may be freestanding, although there are so many mutual benefits to share between a residence and a residential greenhouse that most are attached to houses, or even integrated into them. The primary benefit is heat. Greenhouses can collect substantially more heat than they need for themselves during most seasons of the year, in most sections of the country. That extra heat can be given to the house. A solar greenhouse can be a nice place to sit, if it forms part of a house. Operated properly, it can help to keep household humidity at a healthful and comfortable level year-round. For many reasons—some known, some still under study—solar greenhouses seem able to escape or to solve many of the problems inherent in conventional greenhouses. People who have them and use them, love them. And they can feed you, delivering crisp fresh vegetables regularly just about year-round.

Food is the reason for this book. Greenhouse flower-growers can find many books in print to help them but growers of food in one-household quantities, so far, have had to fend for themselves. Numbers of solar greenhouses are growing so quickly, however, that many of their owners are guaranteed to be new to raising food under glass—and new ventures often do better with a little help.

HOW TO USE THIS BOOK

Your greenhouse is unique. Whether heated by solar energy or other fuels, it is different from your neighbor's, the one down the block or the one across town, for several reasons. Climate varies from one place to the next, even between houses in the same neighborhood. And greenhouses fit into particular sites as well as specific climates. They should be managed to meet these criteria, to function most efficiently. Socrates said, "Know thyself." If you want to make it a rich and blooming producer of all sorts of good things, know thy greenhouse.

Use this book as a set of directions, combined with your greenhouse design and behavior plus local weather, to lead you from one point to the next.

The book is arranged by months. The most valuable function of a food-growing greenhouse is that it extends the seasons—but by doing so it also rearranges them to some extent. Experience in outdoor gardening may be no help at all to the novice greenhouse gardener. (although sensitivity to plants' needs gained outdoors *will* help). By the arrangement, I have tried to indicate greenhouse seasons in a usable way, and to place information near the point at which it would be needed.

Know also thy climate. Extremes of season—the dead of winter in January and the height of summer in July—are likely to be very similar for greenhouses across the country, but at every other time of year solar greenhouses are extraordinarily responsive to local conditions. I have tried to indicate what those are likely to be, with short notes on conditions and chores appropriate to that month at the beginning of each chapter. The weather maps included at the end of the book are intended to contribute to a growing understanding of the cycles of heat and cold, light and dark, that should be part of your greenhouse lore, and should enable you to transpose directions accurately. There will be regions in which instructions given for March, for example, are more appropriate to February. Notes and maps should enable you to determine when things will work in your greenhouse.

Record keeping is an important part of that process. I have tried to include directions for keeping the different kinds of records required, at points where the need for those records will arise during the year.

This book is also arranged, January to December, to put the most vital information first so that the novice greenhouse manager will find the basic principles at the beginning of the book, and the helpful details toward the end. For that reason, the first two chapters deal with environment and microclimate, with information that tells how to study a solar greenhouse to learn every nook and cranny under your glass. Running a greenhouse without this knowledge is like driving a car missing half its cylinders. Plants just will not do as well, and will demand more from you. The knowledge is pleasant to acquire in your own greenhouse: put a chair in it, sit, and listen; assimilate it. If nothing else you will find it an immensely relaxing place to be.

The third chapter, March, explains soils at the point when you are most likely to need them, when the planting year swings into full production.

May begins the discussion of greenhouse seasons. I have defined three basic greenhouse gardens. You will find two of them applicable to your greenhouse. The critical factors that distinguish them are light and heat. The *summer* greenhouse garden probably can be found in every climatic region because it relies on the long days and warm temperatures of the summer months. It will last longer in southern greenhouses than it will in our northerly ones.

The winter garden grows during the short days at the end of the year—in either warm or cool temperatures. Where lots of direct solar radiation keeps greenhouses nice and warm and outdoor temperatures allow it, plants can bloom luxuriously in a *warm winter* greenhouse garden and tomatoes, peppers, herbs, and other warmth-lovers can be raised with relative ease. In the *cool winter* greenhouse garden, however, cool outside temperatures are the rule, and sunlight is diffuse rather than direct. The garden may contain peas, lettuces, Oriental vegetables, brassicas, and the like. The book describes growing conditions for many possible crops so that you can suit the crop to the greenhouse.

After soils, the next most vital bit of greenhouse knowledge probably concerns garden planning. By an arbitrary logic of most-to-least importance it might be in April. But because by gardening logic that would make no sense, planning is where it ought to be, in November when seed catalogs start to bloom and thoughts turn to the coming year, following the record keeping that makes planning easier (October),

preceding sources of help (December). Pest control, essentially any time, is arbitrarily in September.

Along with basic information about solar greenhouses, and directions for climates and crops, this book contains a third kind of information. Many gardeners are experimenters at heart, and enjoy adding adventure and perhaps even romance to the practical pleasures of growing good food. This is for them: Growing fruits and herbs, developing new varieties of plant from saved seed, these are excursions out of the ordinary and are included in those months most likely to provide opportunities to indulge them—April for fruits, June for herbs, August for saving seeds.

Finally, to augment the table of contents and help gardeners with instant needs to find things quickly, there's an index.

When it comes to raising food in solar greenhouses, there are few experts. This book was a direct outgrowth of my own unanswered cries for help, intended to provide the beginnings of a common body of knowledge and to stimulate the development of more. Exchange information with every resource you can find; share experiences with friends and neighbors; invent plants, then spread the word. The more we know, the better equipped we will be to raise our own food and to encourage others to do so.

Delores Wolfe

March 1981
East Swanzey, New Hampshire

CONTENTS

J A N U A R Y

The climate:
dormant across the country, because
days are so short

The chores:
pruning
repotting
preventing whiteflies
tending the salad garden
cleaning and preparation for growth

*J*anuary is generally regarded as a dormant month everywhere. It is too early to start plants for a summer garden, and many of the crops started last summer for fall harvest are past their prime. Yet January is an important month in the solar greenhouse cycle. It is a good time to grow a little salad, to prepare soils for the coming year, to make sure seed flats, pots, and other containers are clean, to prune and repot fruit plants—and to wage war on whiteflies. It is a good month to contemplate the greenhouse environment.

THE GREENHOUSE ENVIRONMENT

In addition to the right soil, temperature and relative humidity, light and ventilation, carbon dioxide (CO_2) and water are important for plant growth. Their effects are interrelated. The greenhouse is a complex environment, and the solar greenhouse is even more complicated by the effects of its design. Scientists are now trying to "dissect" these environments to see how they work in relation to each other and why, and what effect they have on plant growth. Old truths are falling by the wayside as new techniques are tried. All this makes every solar greenhouse grower an experimenter. You may feel like Aristotle crying "Eureka," or like Einstein propounding his Theory of Relativity. It's complex, but if you will take each factor by itself, and study it, all of a sudden the thing works.

1

Light. Of all the factors affecting plant growth, light is the most critical. Plants need light to convert water and minerals to the sugars used in the production of their food. Unless they can produce food to sustain themselves, they cannot grow. Many plants are *photoperiodic:* the length of darkness, or daylight, is critical to proper growth and these requirements may change during the season as the plant goes through successive stages of development. For example, onions require long periods of darkness to turn sugars into food for foliage growth during the spring. As the days become progressively longer, onions will start to form bulbs. (Northern varieties of onions require two to four hours more light per day for bulb formation than southern varieties because northern days are naturally longer than southern days.) Unless onions are planted early enough in the spring to ensure leaves, they will try to grow bulbs without the leaf-derived strength to grow good ones.

Several things happen at night in the plant world. Food produced during the day is used by the plant to increase its size and to grow fruit. Plants also rest at night. Under conditions of continuous light, plants rapidly weaken and become spindly.

Arrange to get all the light you can into the greenhouse, especially in winter. Light quantities and qualities in the solar greenhouse are affected by the type of glazing used on the greenhouse and by the numbers of layers of glazing. Of the light available from the sun, 80 to 90 percent will be transmitted through the first layer of glass. The second layer admits 80 to 90 percent of what remains. The angle at which the sun enters the solar greenhouse also matters. A host of studies have determined the angle of the south wall that lets in the most light for a particular latitude. But the sun changes the angle at which it rides in the sky on a daily basis, so we can have optimum access to solar light infrequently. It is important, then, that the glazing angle be designed to allow optimum light to enter the greenhouse during the period of short days.

There are several ways to enhance the available light

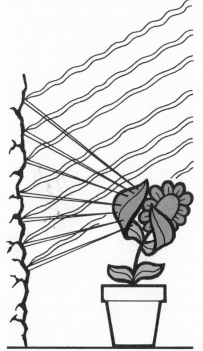

and make it go further. In my greenhouse all absorptive surfaces—heat storage, growing beds, floor area—are dark in color. I want them to absorb light in the form of heat for nighttime use. All other surfaces are painted white or are covered with reflective materials to bounce light into the plants. The north wall (not a heat storing wall in my greenhouse) is covered with crinkled aluminum foil bonded to building paper (available at building supply stores). Part of the greenhouse is insulated with white Styrofoam sheets that also disperse light. The inner layer of glazing consists of sheets of bubble plastic packing material, two layers of plastic bonded together with air trapped in pockets. It is supposed to reduce night heat losses by as much as 30 percent, and it scatters the light so there are fewer dark corners. My plants do not exhibit the spindly growth usually associated with poor light. Some commercial growers are trying light-reflective mulches, such as perlite, or strips of aluminum foil. Aluminum foil may cause hot spots to occur where light is focused into a small area, resulting in leaf burn and other problems related to high temperatures. Crinkled foil on the walls, used to reflect light, can cause the same problem if the light is focused on the growing areas. The north wall of our greenhouse is perpendicular and doesn't seem to concentrate the light strongly enough in any one area to develop hot spots. Some integrated solar greenhouses can use light reflected from adjacent roofs. Some have outdoor reflectors, strips of reflective material arranged to bounce light into the greenhouse. In snowy climates, snow makes a very effective light reflector.

Plants require light in all wavelengths from infra-red to ultra-violet. If they receive too much or too little of any wavelength they will do poorly and may die. In a solar greenhouse where much of the interior surface is used to absorb light for heat, and therefore is dark in color, the quality of light can be degraded.

If plants appear to be spindly, stretching for light, or growing poorly, the problem may be inadequate light. Paint all possible areas white. Consider the use of reflective materials. Do all you can to brighten up your sunspace and make it cheerful—the lighter it is, the better your plants will do.

Temperature. Memories of a summer spent pollinating plants by hand in a greenhouse in Pennsylvania had left me with the feeling that greenhouses were no place to be during the spring, summer, and even fall seasons. The flowers (petunias) thrived, and we wilted. I still cannot look a petunia in the face, and do not grow them. Plants have optimum temperatures at which they do best, although they can take variations to some degree. Most plants (except those with subtropical heritages) do well when temperatures are in the 60° to 70°F range during the day and about 10°F lower at night. Some plants do require a slightly higher temperature when blossoming.

Heat above the optimal temperature can have as bad an effect on plant growth as cold can. Growth slows above 90°F for most plants, and stops when temperatures exceed 95°F for all but a few very heat-tolerant varieties. Plants die when temperatures go above 120° to 130°F. Below 45° to 50°F, growth also slows; it ceases below 40°F. Mature plants often can withstand extreme temperatures better than young seedlings, if they have been gradually hardened to cold (or to heat). Helen and Scott Nearing in Maine, as well as other northern solar greenhouse growers, have found that some cool weather crops can freeze and thaw with no harm to the plant.

Recently (1977), Dr. B.R. Smith found that low air temperatures have much less effect if *soil* temperatures are maintained near optimal growth levels. If soil is cold, the root system will not transport water to the stem and thence to the leaves of a plant for food production. If light is sufficient and the soil is warm, however, the process of photosynthesis can proceed even if the air temperature is cool. In a ground bed, soil temperature will vary somewhat between the top and bottom of the bed and around the sides. The difference usually is not significant. To take the temperature of your soil insert the thermometer at least 2 inches—but no more than

halfway—into the soil, and note the depth at which you take the temperature.

Several things can be done to keep soil temperatures where they should be. The solar greenhouse usually is designed to slow the movement of heat as much as possible, putting and keeping it where it will be most useful. How each greenhouse does this affects exactly how you can use it. Where design leaves off, other methods must begin. Thermostatically-controlled heating coils are available and can be installed under the soil. To function best, the cables should be insulated from the ground below. However, such solid insulations as Styrofoam retard drainage, and fiberglass insulation is not much good when wet. (I have not found a solution to this problem.)

Making the ground bed large enough and keeping it moist will retain more heat and release it slower. Plants that require special heat conditions can be grown best in pots, with heating coils just under them in a special section of the greenhouse. If you do go to the expense of running heating cables, consider covering the heated soil with a canopy of plastic at night to retain more of the heat. Mulch around the plants will also retain soil heat.

When you plan your greenhouse, you might consider terracing the beds or growing plants on top of the storage system. Terracing exposes more material to the sun's light and thus more solar heat is likely to be stored. Especially in

the cool weather greenhouse, it creates more microclimates optimal for plant growth, and it can extend the growing area into the nooks and crannies of the terrace wall. But be careful to keep heat storage walls relatively clear.

In laying out your greenhouse, keep these facts in mind: Benches raise plants into a warmer microclimate—yet they place root systems where they are more directly affected by the vagaries of the weather. A pot of soil has little mass. Ground beds, on the other hand, have a lot with which they can absorb more heat and release it more slowly. To be most effective, build your ground beds so that their surface is about 16 inches above the level of the floor. In addition to providing the best growing space, cold air will tend to move off the beds onto the floor and reduce chances of frostbite for your plants. Ground beds are more ideally suited to the cool weather garden, and benches to the warm weather garden.

Relative Humidity is the measure of water vapor carried in the air. The warmer the air, the more moisture it can contain. As air cools, moisture condenses onto cooler surfaces or it "rains." The relative humidity of the greenhouse should be about 60 percent. If the air becomes too dry for a period of time, plants can wilt and crops will produce seed rather than fruit. Humidity above 70 percent encourages the spread of damping off and other fungus diseases, and promotes the growth of foliage rather than fruit.

Humidity levels can be a real problem where air is normally dry, as it is in the Southwest. Maintaining indoor levels of even 40 percent is hard when outdoor humidity levels hover around 10 percent—especially when, in this section of the country, greenhouses must be ventilated frequently even in winter to prevent heat build-up. The extra heat goes to the house. There are several ways you can regulate humidity. You can increase or decrease the amount of ventilation: increasing ventilation allows you to get rid of excess humidity; reducing it keeps moist air in the greenhouse. You can water the floor and other greenhouse areas. Evaporation puts water into the air rapidly and prevents foliage from drying out. You can add water vapor to the atmosphere without harming plant systems by over-watering ground beds. And you can mist air or foliage to increase humidity levels while, at the same time, you keep leaf tissues moist. If the humidity level is high at all times, ventilate and use fans to keep it within acceptable bounds. On cloudy days or days when temperatures are not high enough to warrant venting, use small fans to keep air stirred around plants. This decreases the humidity around the plant itself, and will reduce the possibility of mold growth.

Ventilation. Ventilation is stressed throughout this book for its effectiveness in controlling humidity, pests and diseases, and temperature. Vents should be opened slightly when daytime temperatures reach 70 °F outside, and opened wider, for longer periods, as temperatures climb higher. As soon as outdoor temperatures stay above 55 °F nights, vents should be left open day and night. If you are not able to vent at the proper times manually, thermostatically controlled vents are available. Kitchen exhaust fans, large wall fans, and the vents at the peak of the greenhouse can all be operated in this manner while you are away from the greenhouse. *But don't blow a gale!* Plants do not mind a gentle breeze, but a strong breeze will dry them out rapidly and greenhouse plants do not have the reserves of water to draw upon that garden plants have outside. Plants in containers will dry out even faster than those in ground beds.

Water is an essential element of the photosynthetic process. It is also the medium by which minerals are transported from the soil to the leaves and other plant parts where they are needed. When water is in short supply, plants modify their needs and get by on less, at the expense of growth. Some plants, such as cacti, survive on a restricted intake for a long period of time. Others, such as lettuces, cannot.

Excessive amounts of water are as harmful as too little. Water replaces the air in soil and the effect on the plant is much the same as drowning. Your fingers are sensitive devices for testing the moisture in soil. You can feel its dampness. There should be no puddles of water on top of the soil on the garden beds, nor should your plants be sitting in puddles. Take care not to splash plant leaves when watering. Dirt can cling to wet leaves and can harbor disease. Use a fine spray and mist the foliage at the same time. Tender seedlings should be watered from below to avoid root damage. Potted plants also can be bottom-watered by placing them in sand-filled trays to which water is added. This keeps the pot and the plant roots out of water, but allows water to siphon up into the pot as needed. This system can be set up to care for your plants while you are away if water can drip slowly onto the tray.

Those who live with chlorinated water should allow the water to set in open buckets (not in the greenhouse) for twenty-four hours before using it on plants. The chlorine gas will dissipate into the air. *Never* use water that has passed through a water softening system or has been otherwise chemically treated. It contains a high concentration of salts that will build up rapidly in the soil and kill the plants. Where well water is used, the temperature of the water may be too cold for tender root systems. Plants prefer water above 50°F, with the optimum being about 75°F—although water that is too warm will harm the roots. Using warm water during cool months also warms up the soil and gets the plants off to a quicker start in the morning.

Try not to water on cloudy days. Plants take up less moisture when less light is available and, because the relative

DRIP WATERER

humidity is apt to be high on cloudy days, less moisture can evaporate from leaves. This may cause mildew or fungus problems. During short winter days, the best time to water is between the hours of 8 am and noon. During long hot summer days, water between 7 am and 3 pm. In dry climates, potted plants may like two drinks each day—they dry out rapidly.

Carbon Dioxide. Plants require differing amounts of CO_2 to make food. On a sunny day the amount of carbon dioxide in the greenhouse atmosphere can decrease rapidly to the point where there is not enough for food production, and while some plants can scrape by with minute quantities of CO_2, others need large amounts. Conventional greenhouses were, until recently, leaky enough to permit an exchange of outside air with inside air that replenished CO_2 rapidly. The use of fossil fuel-burning furnaces also added more of the gas to the greenhouse air. Now, as greenhouses become energy-tight buildings and air infiltration is lessened, commercial growers have found that they must add CO_2 to the air for best plant growth.

Horticulturists have tried a number of techniques to boost CO_2 levels. Most are expensive and could not be adapted easily to the residential greenhouse. I've relied solely on organic methods to solve other problems, and the solution to this may also lie in an organic method.

The New Alchemy Institute has tried composting organic wastes in their greenhouses with some degree of success. Their solution, because it requires four on-going compost piles, is not feasible for small residential greenhouses. But composting does add CO_2 to the air, and heat to the greenhouses. (See page 47.) You can keep such decomposing organic materials as semi-rotted manure in your greenhouse to release carbon dioxide slowly. The process is hastened somewhat by keeping the materials moist, and it will be nearly odorless if you poke holes in the pile with a pitchfork every day or two, although bugs may be a problem if you're not careful. I usually move a trash can full of chicken manure into the greenhouse after the ammonia odor is gone. If brought into the greenhouse in August, the manure will have decomposed sufficiently by January to be used in the ground bed and in the potting mix. Chicken manure is high in nitrogen, so you can use less than cow or horse manure. (Never use fresh chicken manure—it may burn plants.) Hay bales are another good source of CO_2. They will not decompose as rapidly as they would if properly composted, but will provide a low-level, steady supply of the gas. In the spring, when the bales are no longer needed, put them in the compost pile—and watch out for weeds.

Ventilation will improve CO_2 levels. Levels outside the greenhouse are higher, even on sunny days, than inside where plants are soaking it up. If your greenhouse is attached to your house, venting house air into the greenhouse should raise CO_2 levels. In our first indoor growing space (a large bay window) we found that the plants did much better during the winter after we started burning wood for heat. Now, on cold sunny days, we open a window between the house and greenhouse and turn on a small fan. For emergency first aid, Sara Balcomb waters CO_2–starved plants with club soda.

All these measures to enrich the atmosphere with CO_2 will be wasted if the light quality and quantity are not at appropriate levels, or if temperatures are too cold.

The interplay between CO_2 quantities available to plants and the other environmental conditions is complex. All have to be right for photosynthesis to happen. But research is uncovering new ways in which these interactions occur, and solar growers should keep abreast of current gardening news.

WEATHER

The weather outside the greenhouse affects its interior environment, and influences the crops you can grow in it. Weather can vary from one side of town to the other, or from the top of a hill to the valley below. It certainly varies from one region of the country to another, and lends distinctive character to gardens wherever they may be. The greenhouse garden is no exception.

Maps to provide data on average daily outside temperature, hours of sunshine, and the percent of direct solar radiation that you may get for each month in any location in the continental United States would be very useful—and can be found in the appendix on page 178. In all cases, use these maps as *general* guides to your climate. Local variations in terrain, nearness to large bodies of water, and atmospheric conditions will modify the data. Rely on local forecasts and your own knowledge of how your location varies from the local norm, for best information. If you are interested in your local climate contact the National Weather Center, Federal Building, Asheville, N.C. 28801, and ask for detailed weather data for your area. Supply the name of your nearest large airport or city.

RAISING RABBITS AND FISH IN THE GREENHOUSE

For many centuries Oriental farmers have, when possible, raised crops of fish in small ponds to augment their food supplies. Aquaculture on the small farm has now developed into quite a science with fish an integral part of the farm food chain. Fish feed on many different types of food. Some exist nicely on water plants, others on the wastes from water fowl, other fish, and whatever else sinks to the bottom of the pond. And, of course, big fish feed on little fish! By knowing the feeding habits of fish, you can raise several different kinds in one pond, if each kind of fish eats a different food. The New Alchemy Institute people, Jim DeKorne (author of *The Survival Greenhouse*), and others have tried raising fish crops in water storage tanks in their greenhouses. This makes sense in a number of ways. If you store solar heat in water, you have a large body of water sitting there available for other uses as well. This water, if heated by the sun and given an injection of pond water, will produce enough algae to feed some fish. The dark green color of the water containing algae absorbs more heat than similar tanks of clear water. Now, if the fish will grow to sufficient size, you can harvest some organically grown fresh protein. One of the biggest problems

has been to raise enough fish of sufficient size to make it all worthwhile.

Rabbits have also been nominated for greenhouse life. *Rabbits do not belong in the greenhouse!* Those were the first words our friend and rabbit-raiser, Charles Sheaff, said to us when we asked him about it. Rabbits cannot tolerate the temperatures of the greenhouse on bright sunny days—even in January. You never see rabbits gambolling in a field on hot days. They stay in their earth-cooled underground quarters, venturing outside only in the cool of the evening or early morning. If you would like to raise rabbits, try putting a couple of hutches in the garage or build a small shelter for them in the back yard. Then, take the nice rich manure they will give you and place it in shallow bins in the greenhouse. Plant a few earthworms in each bin, and they will chew the manure into compost, adding valuable worm castings to the material. You will have several by-products: good compost, CO_2 for the plants, and a greatly increased population of worms for your gardens and for fishing.

THE SALAD GARDEN

But what about food? What can I grow in a greenhouse when the night temperatures are low–even below freezing during long-lasting cold spells? Most of the cold-loving leafy salad greens do very well in a protected environment and can even stand a little frost. It is possible to reap up to half a pound of greenery each day, if you observe just a few do's and don'ts.

First, grow winter crops in deep ground beds, or large raised growing beds, where soil mass alleviates major temperature swings.

Second, time plantings carefully so that fresh greens are continuously available. Each greenhouse has its own microclimate. For this reason a precise planting timetable is impossible. As a by-guess and by-gosh method, I plant a new succession every three to four weeks depending on the rate at which the vegetables mature (in winter light, growth takes twice as long) and on our demands.

Seeds should be started in flats using some of the pasteurized soil mix described on page 41. When they are big enough to transplant—with two true leaves—move them to the ground bed. I usually keep my flats on top of my heat storage where the barrels help to keep the soil warm and the plants receive about five to six hours of sunlight each day.

The seedlings should be watered every three to four days depending on the amount of sunlight and the water-retaining qualities of the soil. Do not overwater. The soil, when the index finger is inserted into it, should feel moist, not wet.

Chinese members of the cabbage family (brassicas) are very well adapted to cool climates and provide a variety of tastes for salad, soups, and stir-fry dishes. *Bok Choy* is very popular, as are *Gai Choy, Dai Ga Choi, Seppaku Taina,* and *Kyo Mizina.* (See December, **Resources.**)

Leaf lettuces - Buttercrunch, Grand Rapids, Kagran, Oak Leaf and Salad Bowl are hardy and good producers. Grow several types for a variety of color and flavor in the salad bowl.

For continuous harvest, all the green vegetables—lettuces, brassicas, and others—should be harvested as follows: pick the outer leaves and work your way to the center of the plant. Do not harvest the center portion or cut the top of the plant. Grow enough plants so that you can cut no more than two or three leaves from each plant every time you harvest. This lessens the shock to the plant and encourages foliage production.

Endive, chicory, kale, and swiss chard add variety to meals. Chervil and parsley, used as garnishes, and most other herbs, also do well during cold weather.

Snow peas and sugar snap peas (edible pea pods) can be grown in fairly small spaces if trellised. The seeds should be sprouted first (see March for techniques), then planted to a depth of 1 ½ inches in two rows 3 inches on each side of the trellis. Succession plantings timed every two weeks will keep peas available until spring plantings can be made outside.

Vegetable plants bearing fruit, such as tomatoes, may do poorly in the cool greenhouse because they require warm days and nights to set fruit. (For tips see July–**Tomatoes for**

Christmas) Where it is difficult to sustain temperatures of 55°F to 65°F at night, try growing this crop in the house.

Generally, when I order seeds for the outdoor garden in December, I also order my greenhouse seeds. Outdoor varieties, however, may not be very successful in the greenhouse. Much depends upon your greenhouse climate. I tend to select cold-hardy varieties that can withstand temperatures in the low 30°s—even a touch of frost—but do not care for temperatures over 70°F. Seed catalogs should indicate hardiness, or look for crops that are planted and harvested in the spring.

PLANTING TIPS

PAPER CUP COLLAR

Chinese Cabbage: These plants do not take up the space that European cabbages do and, with the excellent selection of varieties, they are a prime candidate for the salad garden. Cabbages are susceptible to club-foot, a slime mold fungus that causes distorted, slimy roots, and that remains in acid soils for a long time. Your best bet to get rid of it is to avoid planting brassicas in the same area each year. To inhibit cutworms, another threat, from slicing off the exposed part of the plant, form a paper collar, made from a bottomless paper drinking cup, around your plant. The top of the cup should be at least ½ inch above the soil.

Chards: A member of the beet family with leaves that taste like spinach, chards can stand widely fluctuating temperatures. Small amounts of space can produce goodly quantities of this vegetable.

Endive: Like lettuce, this vegetable comes in numerous interesting forms, from a broad, almost flat leaf, to one that is tightly curled. Because endive may be slightly bitter or strong to the taste, it should be blanched for several weeks before picking. Gather the leaves together like a topnot and hold in place with string or a large rubber band or, if there is room and you have boxes, just slip them over the plants. Snails like endive leaves and may be a problem. Control with a little table salt judiciously applied. If plant centers are rotted, it may be due to water splashing on the leaves.

Escarole: A form of broad-leafed endive.

Lettuce: Lettuce needs moist humus soils and cool weather. Water frequently in the morning hours, taking care not to splash the leaves. Growth is affected by the amount of available light and temperature. Good ventilation is important to control temperature as well as to reduce the chances of leaf rot. Lettuces can be grown closely together if fans are used to stir the air around them.

The onion family: Leeks, scallions, and chives can be sown closely together. They will grow fairly rapidly from seeds. They are relatively disease-resistant, one of their nicest traits. Garlic is best grown in the summer garden and stored dry for winter use, but if fresh herbs are important, then plant a few cloves. Shallots, another member of this versatile family are easy to grow and provide an interesting garnish.

Peas (edible pod): Also easy to grow, these can be raised in a small space and, if planted in succession, crops will provide a wealth of fresh wintertime food. Trellises can be made of string suspended from the greenhouse glazing bars or from a convenient beam, or chicken wire makes a nice climbing fence. Pick frequently to promote the production of pods.

Spinach: True spinach does not like temperatures much above 50°F, but craves lots of light. New Zealand spinach, however, does do well in the greenhouse and can stand its hottest days.

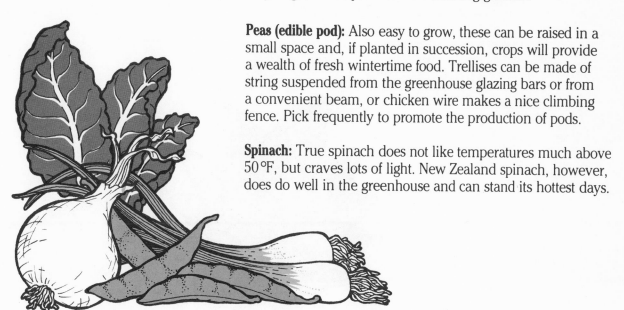

It looks and tastes much like real spinach, and should be grown in large pots or tubs as it requires a lot of room. Sow the seed close together, then selectively thin and eat the tender young plants. Harvest the outer leaves of the mature plant. If watered often the plants will grow profusely but avoid splashing water on the leaves.

Turnips: If harvested while still young and used as a green leaf vegetable, turnips can be grown in a small space with few problems.

Plant	Growing Conditions	Time From Seed to Harvest	Comments
CHINESE CABBAGE	35-60°F plant in square	2½-3 months	Needs rich, moist soil, cool temperatures. Do not transplant.
CHARDS	35-60°F	2 months	Harvest outer leaves. Easy to grow; high in vitamins, minerals.
ENDIVE	45-60°F	7 months	Start late summer for winter crops. Succession planting. Requires special planting techniques.
ESCAROLE	40-65°F	3 months	Very hardy. To blanch heart, cover with box 2-3 weeks.
LETTUCES	45-60°F	2-4 months	Needs ventilation to prevent leaf molds; harvest outer leaves. Leaf lettuces grow best.
ONION FAMILY (LEEKS, GARLIC, SCALLIONS, ETC.)	40-70°F	3-5 months	Leeks & scallions are great winter soup and stew foods. Garlic is slow grower & is better raised in the summer garden.
PEAS, SNOW (EDIBLE PODS)	40-60°F	2 months	Trellising allows good growth in limited space. Pick frequently; plant in succession.
SPINACH	40-50°F	2 months	Needs rich, loose soil, cool weather. Harvest outer leaves frequently; plant in succession.
TURNIPS	45-60°F	greens 1 month roots 2 months	Thin at 5" high for use as greens.

Herbs: *Most perennial herbs can be wintered over in the greenhouse in those areas where the climate is severe. Annuals require a minimum temperature of 45°F to sprout. Start a miniature herb garden in the fall for fresh kitchen herbs.*

Table 1

17

Gardens in Pots,
Containers,
Boxes,
Bushels,
Baskets,
and Barrels

FEBRUARY

The climate:
variable, according to region

The chores:
twiddle the thumbs or
start the seedlings
depending on where
you are

*F*ebruary varies. The weather changes dramatically this month, with winter usually letting those of us in the north have its worst before it bows out. But days are growing longer, and the itch to put trowel in soil is growing. Chores will depend on your greenhouse climate, and may range from simply sitting and twiddling your green thumbs to starting seedlings for the outdoor garden. One way to find out which is to do a little sleuthing. So put on your Deerstalker hat, get out a weather atlas, and see if you can find another spot in the world that has a climate like yours. Sara Balcomb's Santa Fe greenhouse, for instance, is most like San Diego in April; her neighbor's is Atlanta in October. Discover what they grow, and how they grow it, for possibilities in your greenhouse.

MICROCLIMATES

Part of knowing the climate in your greenhouse is to know what its temperature, humidity, and other features are at all times of the year. This involves some record keeping, but is a great way to get family, friends, and neighbors involved in your greenhouse. After taking some measurements and plotting out information, you will find certain areas of your greenhouse that are warm and sunny while others may be cool and sunny, or shady. Each of these areas is a *micro-climate,* a small piece of the larger greenhouse climate that

19

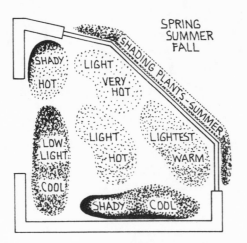

GREENHOUSE MICROCLIMATES

Adapted from *The Food and Heat Producing Greenhouse* by Bill Yanda and Rick Fisher.

can be used more efficiently to grow crops. *Microclimates must be foremost in your plans for all greenhouse growing.* Microclimates, for instance, make it possible for me to grow peppers in a cool greenhouse because there are some nice warm spots in it where they do well. Once we understand microclimates we can take advantage of them, using ground beds, containers, and hanging gardens properly.

Microclimates are small bits of the environment. If you have ever stood in front of a fire with warmth on one side of you and coolness on the other side, you have experienced two microclimates first-hand. Each greenhouse has several and no greenhouse has a set exactly like those of any other greenhouse. Greenhouse microclimates vary with the seasons and with the time of day. Understanding what composes them and how each one acts will help you to raise better crops and may even permit you to grow plants you thought you couldn't.

Just as you can get to know yourself at a great expense through psychiatry and by study, you also can spend a lot of money in sophisticated gadgetry to study your greenhouse–or you can spend a small amount of money and some time, and arrive at the same conclusions. Another demonstration of the "Small is Beautiful" approach, this will teach you things about your greenhouse behavior that can't be picked up by mere electronic sensors.

What sort of equipment will you need?

- Humidistat or a wet/dry bulb thermometer.
- 2 maximum/minimum thermometers, to record air temperatures.
- 2 soil thermometers, to record soil temperatures.
- 1 laboratory thermometer, to take the temperature of your storage system.
- An accurate clock or watch.
- A tape measure or yard stick so you know where your locations are.
- Notebook and record sheets plus some graph paper.
- A light densitometer—if you happen to have a friend that has one you can borrow—to record the amount of light in foot-candles. This is nice, but not essential.

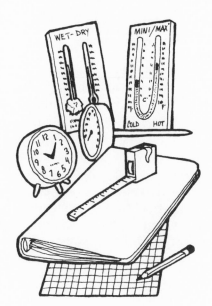

Once you have collected the paraphernalia, set up a schedule for taking the data and recording it, and stick to this schedule as closely as possible. If you cannot because you are going on a trip or out for the day, arrange for someone else to do it or note in your records the fact that you did not take readings that day. If you take readings earlier or later than scheduled, record the time. Then when you plot out the data on a graph, you won't worry about the bump in it. Your schedule can be set up to record data once a day (not of much value), twice a day, or three times daily. I prefer the last.

Next, you should prepare record sheets, adding or eliminating columns as necessary, and have them copied.

The next step is to locate the equipment in your greenhouse in such a manner that you will always know where each piece is. You will need a permanent reference point, one that will not be painted into obscurity or moved. I use a bolt that was incorporated in the foundation when it was poured. From this point I measure, always keeping right angles (no diagonals), to the spot. Note down the directions: so many inches east, so many inches south, etc. If possible, I

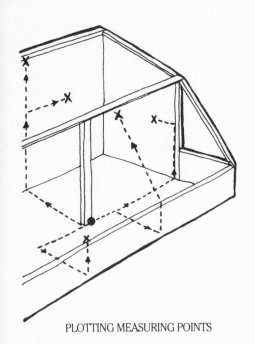

PLOTTING MEASURING POINTS

leave a nail at each location, but nails can be unintentionally pulled out. I change the measuring places about every two weeks, and try to return to each spot four times a year, for information about each area of the greenhouse in each season.

For air measurements, locate one thermometer to the front of the greenhouse and the other toward the back. If one is high, place the other one lower down. I place my soil thermometers so that one is usually in the center of the bed and the other is at one of the ends.

If you are measuring light, you will measure it in a number of locations: high, low, front, back, near the east and west walls, and in the center. The number of readings depends on the size of your greenhouse. David McKinnon, who has contributed significantly to understanding how solar greenhouses work, has found that light will vary considerably within short distances inside the greenhouse. I do not have access to a light densitometer so I note visual observations on the brightness of the sun, number of hours of sunlight in various parts of the greenhouse, and amount of cloud cover or shadow. The information you obtain from the weather maps on page 181 or from the National Weather Center also can be useful.

A humidistat, which measures humidity, works much like a thermostat and, like the thermostat, it can turn a humidifier on and off to maintain a level of moisture in the air. A wet/dry bulb thermometer is a simpler device for finding out the same thing. Two thermometers are attached to a temperature scale. One has a bit of cotton around the bulb that is moistened. The thermometers are twirled and then both temperatures read. The wet bulb temperature will be lower than that of the dry bulb. The temperature readings can be correlated on a chart that comes with the thermometer to find the relative humidity percentage.

You will want to place your humidistat next to the maximum/minimum thermometer. Eyeballing humidity is difficult at best. You can start the morning with 100 percent humidity and by noon be down to 40 percent humidity—or vice versa. Because humidity is a function of temperature, the amount of moisture the air can hold depends on how hot the air is. If the air in your greenhouse is too dry, your plants will not be as perky as they should be, and the leaves will feel dry.

Once you have started collecting the data, you will want to interpret it. You can simply look for trends, such as which locations stay above 55°F at night, or you can plot them on a graph. This is not difficult and will often show a trend you might otherwise miss. I graph the information for each location on one piece of graph paper, so that all the information about a particular location is handy on one sheet.

The trends shown on the graphs should allow you to select microclimates suitable to the growth of certain crops. For example, the area in the center of your greenhouse, 1 foot below the rafter, might be ideal for the fall tomato crop in hanging planters. Spinach, a cool weather crop, might do well in the center front of the ground bed where it gets maximum sunlight, but temperatures are cooler. You can shift your plants with the seasons to keep them in their optimum climates. For this reason, the more finicky plants are grown in containers.

Microclimates must be carefully considered when planning the garden layout. Using the knowledge you have gained about how your greenhouse functions, you should be able to adapt your gardens better to conditions as they exist during each phase of the yearly cycle of growing.

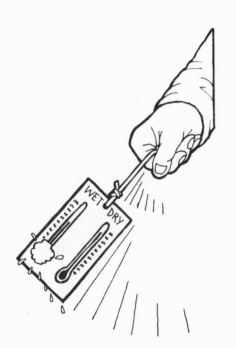

TAKING HUMIDITY READINGS

HOW TO FILL OUT THE RECORD SHEET

Time: Enter the time when you take your readings. If you take readings several times each day, enter each set of readings on a separate line.

Daily Maximum/Minimum: Once each day record the maximum and minimum temperature of the greenhouse. If you are using several max./min. thermometers and the readings vary in different locations, be sure to include the reading for each location on an expanded chart.

Date	Time	Outside Temp. °F Max. Min.	Air Temp. °F Loc. 1	Loc. 2	Loc. 3	Soil Temp. °F Loc. 1	Loc. 2	Percentage Humidity	Light	Weather	Comments

SAMPLE DATA CHART

Air temperature: Record the temperature at the various locations. The number of columns will be determined by the number of thermometers you have.

Soil Temperature: The same as air temperature.

Percent of humidity: If you have a wet/dry bulb thermometer, you can read and enter the relative humidity.

Light: Without a light densitometer, you should establish some sort of criteria to record the *amount of sunlight.* Note the sharpness of shadows cast by a particular object, such as a post. Weather conditions will also provide clues. Remember to record the *length of time* for each different light condition you observe.

Weather: It is important to note such conditions as amount of cloud cover, sky conditions (clear, hazy, etc.), outdoor temperature, if possible, and wind. The Beaufort Wind Scale may be found in the Appendix on page 187.

Comments: Include here any pertinent information that might affect the environmental conditions, and thus the growing conditions, of the plants. Such items as blossoms dropped by pepper plants are indicators that temperature conditions were poor where the plant had been located.

MOVABLE GARDENS

Container gardening is one way to make good use of your microclimates, and you can easily move plants from outside to greenhouse and back again as the seasons progress, or into the house if it becomes necessary. Most of the fruits and vegetables we discuss in this book can be grown in containers. There is no big challenge to this form of gardening—in fact, it can be easy and quite a lot of fun to seek out different types of containers.

A few pointers: First, plants in containers must have at least five hours of full sunlight. Such plants as tomatoes and spinach will require more. The important thing to remember is: unless a plant likes shade, keep it in full sun and not in the shadow of other plants. This can be done by using narrow shelving for container gardens, or a step-like arrangement on which to set the pots, with the taller ones toward the back.

The plants should not be crowded together. Crowding cuts down on air circulation and may cause disease problems. It is very easy to push the pots together, so as an additional precaution I may turn on a small fan to stir the air above the plants.

Moisture can be a problem in containers if you have not allowed enough drainage holes around the base of the recep-tacles. On very large containers, I drill 1-inch holes every 5 to 6 inches around the bottom edge, and several in the bottom itself. Be sure to place the holes where they will not be plug-ged by whatever the pot stands on. I sometimes also put a 1-inch layer of coarse gravel in the bottom of very large con-tainers to promote drainage. Adequate drainage is important because containerized plants are watered frequently. Water has to be able to get out of the bottom of the pot or soggy soil conditions will cause root rot. A dish or pan under the pot should catch the drips, especially where plants overhang other garden areas and the drippings may harm the plants below. A container sitting in the water that drains from the bottom of the pot is an open invitation to root rot and mildews as well as to slugs and snails, so large containers should be raised on bricks placed under the bottoms of

the pots. Such containers as half-barrels and wooden pails should not be allowed to sit on the rims, their weakest parts.

Items used for containers should be a constant challenge to your ingenuity. They can be as simple as milk cartons cut in half lengthwise, or as elegant as something cast in concrete or artistically modeled from clay. I've even used papier mache egg cartons when starting a lot of seedlings. I prefer rectangular wooden containers in which I can grow a variety of plants to make miniature gardens. Wood breathes more naturally than plastic or glazed ceramic wares, and fits in nicely with the rest of my greenhouse. Whatever you use, be sure it is large enough to hold the plant or plants you want to grow in it. For mature plants, such as lettuces and many low growing herbs, the container must be 8 inches deep to provide an adequate base. Larger plants, such as tomatoes and peppers, need 2-gallon size pots that are 12 inches high. Table 2 gives the sizes of the pots recommended for most common vegetables.

If you use half-barrels or tubs, be sure they have not had chemicals stored in them, and that the wood has not been treated with creosote. If you must use a wood preservative, use Cuprinol. Old wine and whiskey barrels are excellent. Both redwood and cedar resist damage by termites and stand up to moisture better than other woods. Before using any container for your garden, scrub it out well with a wire brush and warm soapy water. Then soak it in a solution of one part Clorox and ten parts water for at least twenty minutes. Allow the pot to sit overnight to be sure all the chlorine evaporates. All white discolorations, caused by salts from fertilizers, must be scrubbed away. If the salts cannot be removed, discard the container.

Wooden, clay, and other pots made from porous materials should be soaked in water before being used. Otherwise the container will draw the moisture out of the soil, and the plant will be off to a bad start.

The standard greenhouse 1-1-1 soil mix (page 40) is fine for container gardening. It allows fast draining, retains water well without becoming soggy, provides a good base for the root system, and is not too heavy for root crops. I do mulch with peat moss, vermiculite, or well-rotted compost around the tops of the pots to help keep moisture in.

If you are growing plants that will need support, it is best to place this in the pot before you plant. If you insert staking materials after the plant has been growing for a time, you may damage its root system. Trellises can be nailed into the side of the container if it is wooden, or can be held in place by the planting medium.

When potting or repotting a containerized vegetable, leave enough room between the top of the soil and the rim of the pot to hold the amount of water the plant needs. For small plants, 1 inch is enough, but larger plants will need 1½ to 2 inches of clearance.

Water is crucial to containerized plants. The soil should be equally moist throughout the container. With a fast-draining soil, you should water each plant by hand until water comes out the drainage holes, using a hose or watering can so that the needs of each plant can be met.

It is easy to damage the root systems of potted plants if the spray from the nozzle is too strong. Use a misting or water-breaker nozzle on the hose or watering can. Don't forget to mist the foliage, too, to keep leaf tissues moist.

The moisture content of the soil in container gardens can change rapidly. In dry greenhouses, plants that were adequately moist in the morning may be dry by the afternoon. Check the soil of each pot for moisture content in the morning and, if necessary, again in the afternoon. To help keep the humidity high, water the floor of the greenhouse plus any other surfaces that can be watered. This can be done several times a day if necessary, and will be less bother than having to water dry plants in the late afternoon.

Plants grown in containers need more frequent feeding than those grown in ground or other beds. They start with a limited amount of food and cannot grow roots to seek out additional supplies. To provide a steady diet, top-dress the pots with compost containing a little added lime when you repot the plants. The top dressing should be changed annually for

most fruit trees, and semi-annually for faster growing, heavily harvested fruits and vegetables. Keep an eye on the foliage of vegetables. If it starts turning yellowish-green or yellow (an indication of nitrogen deficiency) feed with dilute fish emulsion. Heavy nitrogen users should have a little bone meal added to their compost. You also can fertilize regularly with dilute liquid fish emulsion applied during watering. For container gardens, use 1½ teaspoons per gallon of water, and apply twice as often as you would if the plant were growing in a bed or in the garden. Because container plants are watered more frequently, nutrients wash out of the soil faster.

When it is cool in the greenhouse, you must watch the temperature of the soil in containers. Roots systems are more prone to suffer from the vagaries of environmental changes because they are closer to the surface of the pots. If your greenhouse tends to remain on the cool side, consider sinking the pots in straw or hay to shield against the cold, or dig them into sand or soil.

When selecting vegetables for container gardens, keep a few things in mind. First: you want crops that will make the effort worthwhile. Second: they should be crops able to do well in a confined space, and will probably be determinant. Determinants have set growth patterns that tend to keep them small. Third: look for varieties that do not require a lot of support. Many seedspeople now feature special varieties suited to containerized growth. Table 0 lists container crops tried by David Lyon and described by him in the May/June, 1980 *New Roots* magazine.

PLANT	CONTAINER & SPACING	VARIETIES
Beans	8" deep, 4" wide per plant Thin to: Bush: 8" Pole: 9-12" Lima: 4-6"	**Snap bush:** Tendercrop, Topcrop, Green-sleeves **Wax bush:** Pencil Pod Wax, Burpees Brittle Wax **Pole:** Kentucky Wonder, Blue Lake, Ramona **Lima:** Fordhook 242, Henderson Bush, King of the Garden
Broccoli Cauli-flower	5 gal. soil or 12" pot per plant Fertilize often	**Broccoli:** Green Comet, Spartan Early, Italian Green Sprouting, De Cicco **Cauliflower:** Early Snowball, Snow King Hybrid, Snow Crown Hybrid, Purple Head
Brussel Sprouts	5 gal. soil or 12" pot per plant Fertilize often	Jade Cross Hybrid, Long Island Improved
Cucumber	2 gal. of soil or 8" pot Thin to 4" apart if growing up on trellis or stakes	Pot Luck, Patio Pik, Burpless Early Pik, Crispy Salty, Tiny Dill Cuke *(first 15-20 blossoms are male and will drop)*
Eggplant	5 gal. soil per plant or 12" tub Space 12" apart	Slim Jim, Ichiban, Black Beauty, Long Tom, Jersey King Hybrid
Pea	6" long box per plant	Alaska, Little Marvel, Frosty, Green Arrow **Snow peas:** Dwarf Gray Sugar, Burpee Sweet Pod **Cowpeas:** Early Ramshorn Black Eye *(keep picked or blossoms stop)*
Pepper	2 gal. soil per plant Space 24"	**Sweet:** Bell Boy, Keystone Resistant, Yolo Wonder **Hot:** Red Cherry, Long Red Cayenne, Jalapeno
Spinach	4" wide by 4" deep per plant Space to 5-6 "	Melody, Longstanding Bloomsdale, America
Squash	5 gal. soil per plant Space 16-24"	**Summer:** Aristocrat, Chefini, Greyzini, Hybrid Zucchini, Patty Pan, Scallopini **Winter:** Gold Nugget, Table King, Banana *(grow on trellis, put fruit in sling)*
Tomato	2 gal. soil per full-sized plant; 6" pot for compact plants	Patio, Pixie, Tumblin' Tom, Small Fry VFN, Better Boy VFN, Early Girl, Salad Top, Super Fantastic VFN, Sunripe VFN, Toy Boy, Tiny Tim *(staking aids yield)*

Table 2

29

M A R C H

The climate:
the start of the growing year,
even though things are already growing
in many places

The chores:
planting and dealing with seedlings . . .
and soils;
planning for warm-weather greenhouse
plants;
and making compost

*M*arch is traditionally the beginning of the gardening year. In days not too long ago—before the time of Julius Caesar—the growing year started with the vernal equinox. March 21 was the beginning of the new year. Many countries still note this tradition in their calendars. It is a time of awakening, and the beginning of the planting season. It may be the busiest time of the year in the solar greenhouse, where seedlings are started for the summer garden outside.

Planting schedules for the greenhouse are arranged to coordinate with the time you traditionally set out the outdoor garden in your area. The April full moon is considered by many in the northeast as the time to plant all the early crops out-of-doors. The full garden is planted in June.

The latest in the country, New Englanders start seedlings in March and make all preparations for the step outside. If you have never before gardened, ask those in your area who have, or consult the gardening editor of your local paper for the right date for you.

PROPAGATING SEEDS

One of the easiest methods of propagating plants, and almost the only method used to raise vegetable plants, is the sowing of seeds. The seed form of sexual reproduction results from the fertilization of the female ovum by the male pollen. Plants raised from seed represent the combined genetic heritage of both parents. Hybrids result from the cross-pollination of two different species of varieties of plant, accidently or deliberately, and tend to emphasize particular characteristics of a plant type. Seeds from hybrid plants will seldom reproduce the traits of the parents and may even be sterile. (For this reason, it is best not to save seeds from hybrid plants.)

Sowing seeds is a simple matter. Most of us have cast seed upon soil and watched a plant grow—in school where the seed was sown in a paper cup full of soil, in our parents' garden, or in our own. Wherever it occurs, and however world-experienced we may be, the first sign of greenery peeping above the soil is still a joyous occasion.

Growing seedlings is a relatively simple procedure. The same general rules hold true for all vegetable crops. If you follow them, you should have no problem in raising goodly numbers of seedlings easily.

RULES FOR GROWING SEEDLINGS

1. Provide the right environment: soil, light, water, temperature, and other environmental conditions set the stage for the future health of the plant and thus directly influence yield.

2. Plant the seed right: struggling up through the soil is a difficult proposition for some seedlings, especially those that take a long time to germinate.

3. Transplant the seedling: the medium in which seeds are germinated has no food. The only nutrients available are

those contained in the seed, so transplant seedlings as soon as possible to give them a good start.

4. Harden seedlings: always adapt seedlings to a new environment gradually. It takes time to become acclimated.

5. Move them outside at the proper time: the wait—both to sow seeds and to move seedlings—can be agonizing, but for the seedling, moving into a new climate is difficult enough without the added shock of adverse climate.

Environment. Because you can control the greenhouse growing environment to sprout most of the seeds you plant, you will sow fewer seeds than if you were planting directly outdoors. Most seeds require consistent temperature and humidity conditions, in order to germinate. To satisfy these demands, plan to germinate your seeds in a propagation flat placed in a propagation box. The propagation flat is simply a seed flat or other container filled with one of the soil mixes described on page 39. The propagation box may be a box as described on page 86, or it may be a sheet of glass or plastic placed over the seeded container so that moisture cannot escape. The propagation flat can also be enclosed in a plastic bag, but take care that the bag does not rest on the soil or the seedlings may rot as they pop through. Poke a few pencil-sized holes in the plastic to allow excess heat to escape. Plastic is nice for those seeds requiring a long germination time because air can pass through the bag but moisture cannot. Place the propagation box where it will receive the temperature and light required by that particular crop.

Germination and growth temperatures used throughout this book are soil temperatures. It has been established that soil temperature is more critical than air temperature, and that some plants can do quite well in a cool climate as long as their feet are warm. Soil temperatures for germination can be closely controlled in a propagation box if you use a thermostatically controlled heating cable under the box. If you have no electricity in the greenhouse, or prefer not to use

PROPAGATION BOX

additional energy, place the flats on top of your free standing heat storage (if you have it), on top of large stones that have been lying in the sun or in front of a sun-bathed masonry wall.

Many fruiting plants must have a warmer temperature to set fruit than is necessary for their growth. Crops such as the brassicas will set inferior fruit if kept at consistently low temperatures in the adolescent growth stage.

I quite often propagate my seeds in a south window during the late fall and winter. As soon as the seedlings have sprouted, I move them to a cooler, but brightly lighted window for a few days before moving them into the greenhouse. House windows can become cold at night, so be sure to provide some protection for seedlings.

Seeds. Select seeds for your outdoor garden that are adapted to its climate. Best results are usually obtained by purchasing seeds from seed companies raising stock in a climate similar to yours. Check temperature and light requirements, particularly for the fall-winter-spring greenhouse in the northern half of the country.

Because your greenhouse can be used to extend your growing season, try raising crops that require a longer season than you normally have outdoors: perhaps sweet potatoes or peanuts, or tropical vegetables. Crops can be scheduled to avoid major bug seasons in the outdoor garden, and the greenhouse can make a two-crop-a-year garden possible. Start cucumbers, melons, and all the marigolds and nasturtiums that will be used as bug repellers in the outside garden. Raising seedlings in the greenhouse gets your garden off to a good start and allows you to select the more vigorous plants. It is expensive to discard weak seedlings purchased from a commercial grower—and just as expensive, in terms of effort, to grow poor plants when you raise your own.

If you will be using your greenhouse during the warm weather of summer, extra effort in keeping the greenhouse below 95°F will be rewarded with a good harvest. Light levels in some solar greenhouses are actually lower in summer, so be aware of light as well as shading needs. Plan to purchase your seeds from seedspeople located further south, if possible, to take advantage of heat-tolerant stock.

Soil. A mixture of one part sphagnum moss to one part sand or vermiculite, with one handful of well-rotted compost worked into each 2 quarts (packed), should be mixed with the hands to reduce all lumps, then moistened thoroughly. But do not soak this mix or you will reduce the oxygen available to the roots. Place the mix in the propagation container and tamp it evenly but, again, not so tightly that most of the oxygen is squeezed out. This mix provides an easier path through the medium for growing roots than traditional mixes, including soil, do.

The mix should fill the container to within 1 inch of the top. Sow the seeds thinly on top. Very small seeds, such as leeks and lettuce, should just be patted in. Larger seeds are covered by the soil mix to a depth three to four times their diameter. Lightly tamp the covering in place.

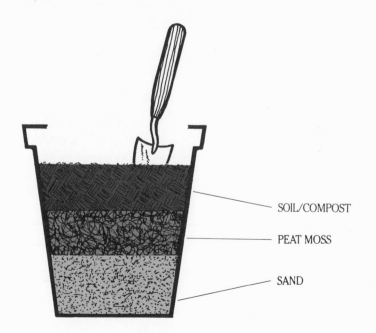

SOIL/COMPOST

PEAT MOSS

SAND

Commercial soilless mixes are also available for germinating seeds. But seedlings will grow, given the right
temperature and humidity conditions, in plain sphagnum
moss, vermiculite, or sand, so I don't see the need to pay a
special price for a propagation mix. Commercial users prefer
them because quality is supposed to be consistent, an important consideration when raising crops for the market.

The standard 1-1-1 sphagnum moss/garden loam/inert
material mix, used for the greenhouse bed and pots, can also
be used to propagate plants. If you do use it, sow seeds very
thinly because you need not transplant as soon as germination
has finished. This is a heavier growing medium than the
sphagnum moss and sand mix, so it is best not to use it
with plants that germinate with difficulty.

Plants outdoors must contend with the vagaries of nature.
Be sure to start enough seedlings to meet your needs as well as
those of natural predators like birds and insects. If you have
extra vegetables at the end of the season, you can store them,
give them away, or rent a booth at the local farmer's market,
but at least you will not go hungry. Most seed catalogs will tell
you how many plants to expect from a packet of seeds, or how
many feet of row you can plant. U.S. Department of Agriculture
Bulletin No. 202, *Growing Vegetables in the Home Garden,*
(available free in single copies from your congressman) provides tables on the amount of seed or plants required to plant
100 feet of row. This booklet also gives the latest dates to plant
spring crops and the earliest dates to start fall crops, as well as
other good information.

When I first started gardening, I found a copy of Charles
Nissley's *The Pocket Book of Vegetable Gardening* (Pocket
Books, Inc., 1942) in a second-hand book store. For each
vegetable, he lists the harvest that can be expected from a
100-foot row of plants. Most seed packets will sow either 100
feet of row or an even fraction of it, so it becomes easy to
calculate the amount to plant, although our family seems to eat
in different quantities from the Department of Agriculture's im-
aginary family. Nissley's book is also full of nice little hints for
raising a garden inexpensively.

Growth temperatures. Once the sprouts have all popped through the soil, move the flats to an area that receives good light and has a constant soil temperature about 10°F less than that used for germination.

Transplanting. I transplant seedlings when they have their first two true leaves. They often suffer less trauma from the shock of moving at this stage than they do at later stages. An important rule to make the move as painless for the plants as possible: have their new home ready in advance and use a transplanting fork. Then, as soon as each has been moved, water it thoroughly.

The transplanting fork can be made by whittling the tapered end of a wooden plant label to a sharp point. Cut a small triangular piece out of the sharp point, and your fork is ready. Be sure to clean this tool after use to avoid spreading disease.

To prepare the transplant medium, take some of the 1-1-1 soil mix and place it in the new container. This should be firmed in place to within 1 inch of the top of the pot. Moisten thoroughly. Take a pencil and open a hole in the soil sufficiently deep to take the new roots—about 1½ inches. With the transplant fork, loosen the soil around the seedling in the germination flat and then lift it out. Place it in the prepared hole and very gently tamp the earth around it using the eraser end of a pencil. Place a light dusting of dry peat moss around the transplant to act as a mulch.

If you are transplanting directly to a bed, loosen the soil in the selected location, water it, cultivate it again, then plant as you would in a container.

New seedlings may not be able to tolerate large doses of sunlight in their first few days, so shade them: a thin layer of straw, a location under a tall plant that will shade them part of the day, or a small potted plant placed in front of them. Those planted in containers can be shifted from shade to sun. If you do not have time for this, be sure to shade these plants as well. Once adapted to their new environment, the seedlings can do without shade.

A TRANSPLANTING FORK

Fertilizing. Transplants should be fed regularly. The faster these plants grow, the more food they will require. Like small children growing into their teens, they will be hungry for those foods that supply the necessary vitamins and minerals. Teenagers seem to get theirs from endless milk shakes and hamburgers. Plants like liquid manure teas and liquid fish emulsion. During this period of fast growth, apply dilute solutions of one of these fertilizers every two weeks. Doing it by hand allows you to dose each plant selectively according to its needs. Some plants (see the chart on page 52) require little fertilizer while others like a goodly portion.

Light and shading. During the fall and winter months we scrounged for all the light we could get. Now, as spring progresses, it may become necessary to screen out some of the sunlight. It may be too intense for tender plants and even for some of the mature ones. This more intense light can raise the temperature in the greenhouse past acceptable limits.

Properly designed solar greenhouses seem to have less trouble with excessive sunlight than conventional glass houses. The angle of the south glazing on many deflects a large portion of direct solar radiation—the source of heat. Opaque north and west walls as well as the roof add to built-in shading. The result is a light bright enough for crops but not strong enough to cause damage.

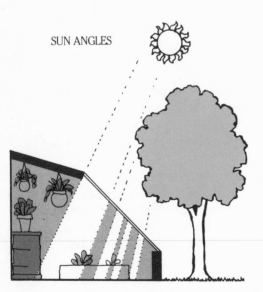

SUN ANGLES

SUMMER SUN

WINTER SUN

Shade trees outside and shrubs that are bare of leaves in the winter and in full leaf by late spring should be considered. An extra benefit from such a tree is the cooling effect it has as water evaporates through its leaves.

A friend of mine picks up slatted porch shades at yard sales and auctions. These provide a dense shadow fine for shade–loving plants but not good for plants that need light. You also may have areas that are permanently shaded during the hot season—as I do—and can use these to raise a summer indoor garden.

Screening nets can be purchased through most of the larger seed companies. When spread over the outside of the glass and well anchored against the wind, they will effectively block out a percentage of the light.

Commercial shading sprays, such as whitewash, are available through greenhouse suppliers and farm and garden stores. They are supposed to wash off, for the most part in summer rains, but they can be difficult to clean off if the rain is insufficient. Remember that, come fall, you want maximum sunlight in your greenhouse again, so try ways that may not entail balancing across your glass, scraping off whitewash or diluted latex paint.

SOILS FOR THE SOLAR GREENHOUSE

In keeping with our stress on organic gardening, soils used in the greenhouse must be free of artificial fertilizers, herbicides, and insecticides. Healthy, balanced soils will result in vigorous plants and will reduce the need for any harmful chemicals.

Soils are composed of many kinds of such inert materials as sand, silt, clay, and stones, combined in varying degrees with organic materials. Organic materials are beneficial as a source of nutrients, as a sponge to absorb water and nutrients, and as a structural element—especially important for sufficient space for air and water movement. When you are collecting soil for large beds, remember that it is easier to rejuvenate a sandy soil than one that is clayey.

Greenhouse soils should start out lighter in weight and

texture than garden soils because the frequent irrigation tends to compact them, but unless your greenhouse soils contain earthworms, they will not be as capable of natural regeneration of some of the nutrients as outdoor soils are. For this reason, it is wise to start with rich soils that can absorb future additions of organic fertilizers. This entails mixing them and adding the necessary ingredients in proper proportions. Most greenhouse recipes are basically the same: 1 part good garden soil and compost, 1 part sphagnum moss, and 1 part coarse sand, ver-miculite, or perlite. Natural organic fertilizers can be added to this basic mix to suit the diet of each crop.

Once the basic mix is prepared, the soil should be tested to determine acidity. Commercially available soil test kits can be used or several soil samples can be tested through your state agricultural extension service. Proper soil acidity is im-portant in maintaining a good organic diet for your plants. It promotes chemical reactions so that plant roots can absorb nutrients, and beneficial bacteria can decompose the organic matter into plant food. Soil acidity is defined by pH—the amount of calcium in the soil that is available to plants. The more calcium, the less acid is the soil. A neutral, pH 7 soil, is neither acidic or alkaline. Optimum greenhouse soils have a pH 5 to 6.5. Frequent watering or irrigation of greenhouse plants tends to leach calcium out of the soil and make it relatively acid. It is best to check pH every few months, especially if your water supply is excessively acid. In the form of lime, or gypsum, calcium can be added to the greenhouse soil mix to raise the pH. Alkaline soils, a major problem in the west, can be acidified with cottonseed meal, or aluminum sulfate.

There is a great difference of opinion about sterilizing greenhouse soils, when careful maintenance of organic-based soils should eliminate the need for this purification method. Being an organic gardener, I opt for the more natural way. Sterilizing soil leaves a product devoid of life, even those good bugs necessary to plant health. Pasteurization, less lethal, gets rid of nematodes and certain other pests without killing off all the good bacteria, but is a terrible thing to go through.

The following pasteurization process will kill most harmful organisms, weed seeds, and pests. Tools required include your oven, a large flat pan with sides several inches high, an oven meat thermometer, and some aluminum foil. Place the soil in the pan to within almost an inch of the top of the pan. Cover with aluminum foil and carefully insert the thermometer through the foil, making sure the thermometer does not touch the bottom or sides of the pan. Place in a 350°F oven until the thermometer reads 180°F. Leave the covered pan in the oven for thirty minutes with heat turned off. Sand, peat moss, vermiculite, and perlite are already sterile. Composts and organic fertilizers will be pasteurized if compost temperatures reach 160°F. Only the soil needs attention. When the process is complete, carefully store any soil not immediately used in a tightly sealed plastic bag from which most of the air has been removed.

I guess the best rule of thumb is to use pasteurized soils to start seedlings in flats, pots, or other containers; otherwise use the unpasteurized soil mix.

Soil nutrients provide most of the basic food elements required for plant growth. There are three key elements—nitrogen, potassium, and phosphorus—plus a host of trace minerals. A shortage of one element will upset the balanced plant uptake of the other two, and can result in a complexity of plant nutritional deficiencies.

Nitrogen, the basic chemical needed to produce plant protein, is abundant naturally but must be converted into a form plants can use, a process that depends on a delicate balance between acidity and bacterial activity. Commercially available pure nitrogen fertilizers can easily upset this balance, causing severe damage to the plant roots. With adequate organic nitrogen, plants grow vigorously, mature on schedule, and their foliage is a nice dark green. Where nitrogen supplies are insufficient—or where bacterial activity is hampered—plant leaves become yellowish and will be small. Excessive nitrogen results in weak, disease-prone plants and an abundance of poor-quality foliage.

In the organic garden, compost and mulches are slowly

decomposed by bacteria, and nitrogen compounds undergo a number of changes. Because the release of nitrogen from organic fertilizers is slow, plants have access to it for a longer period of time and require fewer feedings. Organic fertilizers do not burn the plants, or lead to excessive, weakening growth.

Certain plants, legumes (peas and beans) and certain grasses like clover and alfalfa, have the ability to fix nitrogen in the soil. Bacteria living in nodules on the roots of these plants can digest nitrogen compounds, turning them into nitrates. These nitrates are in a form usable by most plants. Rotating legumes with other crops in the greenhouse will add nitrogen to the soil. Planting legumes near crops requiring large quantities of nitrogen will reduce the need to feed more.

Manures, bone and blood meals, fish and seaweed emulsions, and chopped plant materials are good sources.

Phosphorus is essential for plant vigor, development of the root system, transport of nutrients from root to leaf, and enhancement of disease resistant tendencies. Phosphorus deficiencies should be suspected if plants stop growing and developing. Leaves and stems will turn red-purple in an early warning sign. Where organic composts are used, phosphorus is usually readily available, and deficiencies seldom occur. However, because the solar greenhouse is intensely planted, such organic fertilizers as manure tea or liquid fish and seawood emulsions should be used regularly. When working on the beds, add ground rock phosphate with the composted material. Recommended amounts vary. I use about 8 pounds in my 75 square foot bed, an amount that will last several years. As you add soil to the ground bed, be sure to add a little to keep levels where they should be.

Potassium contributes to the vigor of plants and to their capacity to resist disease. It also acts to buffer the plant against such adverse climatic conditions as drought and cold. Deficiencies cause reduced harvests. Watch for yellow streaking or spotting of leaves and dry leaf tips. If you suspect potassium deficiency, dig up a plant and check the roots. The root system will be poorly developed.

Organic materials such as hardwood ash and compost contain large amounts of potassium. This is generally not sufficient, however, for rapidly growing, densely planted crops. Because our soil is naturally rather acid, I add two pails of wood ash to the ground bed as I re–dig the soil. Greensand or granite dust also will release potassium slowly and continuously over a period of time. Potash, wood ashes, greensand, and granite dust are also rich in essential trace elements.

A word of caution. Potassium minerals, like calcium, will raise the pH of your soil. Add no more than is necessary to supply the mineral, then check the soil pH. If necessary, acidify with a little aluminum sulphate.

Trace minerals such as sulphur, iron, magnesium, boron, manganese, zinc, copper and molybdenum, are necessary for good plant nutrition, but deficiencies may be hard to detect using a

soil test kit. As part of the yearly refurbishing of the greenhouse, send soil samples from various parts of the greenhouse ground bed to your state agricultural agent for analysis. Most trace elements are added naturally with compost, fish meal, bone meal, manure, and liquid fish emulsion, so regular applications of these should suffice.

ORGANIC FERTILIZERS FOR THE GREENHOUSE

Aged manures are worth their weight in gold and, if you have a ready source, you are indeed fortunate. Plant food quality in manures ranks from rabbit and pig manures at the top to horse manure somewhere near the bottom. Rabbits, chickens, and goats are among the more efficient digesters and so have few seeds passing through their intestinal tracts. Their manures are very high in nitrogen as well as other necessary chemicals, and are rich enough to warrant spreading more thinly than some of the other manures. Poultry manures tend to be very high in uric acid and ammonia, however, and if not properly aged and carefully applied, can burn the plants.

If you happen to be on a small or suburban-sized farm, rabbits are great animals and could be the foundation of a profitable little business. They require little space in a shed, garage, or barn. The manure is an added bonus: it can be composted in the greenhouse, contributing heat, fertilizer, and CO_2 to its environment. Rabbits may be just the ticket to good plant health in the easiest possible way.

If sheep and cow manure is what is available, don't turn up your nose! This manure does have good plant food value and has lots of nice humus. My only hassle with cow manure has been the fact that it has to age, unless actively composted, for at least three to four years and even longer if the pile is too big. On the farm, where time is at a premium, manures are allowed to compost with minimal human intervention.

And then there is horse manure. After my experience one summer a few years back, I decided I'd have to be pretty desperate to use it again. In the fall we had the garden profusely manured with year-old composted horse manure. Next spring the garden was plowed and we planted. Only thing was that the weed seeds, never digested as they passed through the horse, also grew. That summer was a constant war. We finally decided to weed around the plants and *mow* between the rows! Always compost fresh manure. Take a tip from us.

If you do not have a good source of manure available, there are other options open to you. Grass clippings, food waste, tree leaves, and any other *clean* (free from chemical contamination) organic material will work.

Most garden stores now carry a variety of organic plant foods that should be part of your garden equipment. Bone meal is a good, slow-acting additive that supplies some nitrogen plus a large quantity of phosphates. Steamed bone meal is taken up by the plants more rapidly than the raw kind, but both are so slow to get to the root system that it is best to work them carefully into the soil around each plant.

Lime, ground limestone, and wood ashes are great for the garden. All tend to sweeten the soil but in differing ways. Lime adds calcium while wood ashes add potassium and phosphorus. Incinerator ashes should be used with some caution.

They are derived from paper products, garbage, boxes, and whatever else goes out with the trash. Sometimes there will be too much calcium or sodium in the ash residue. It can turn the soil alkaline.

If you live near a cannery or food processing plant and have alkaline soil, try to obtain some of their wastes. Because you are adjusting soils more frequently, have soil pH checked more often.

Sawdust is a good, inexpensive soil enhancer that helps in several ways. It can be used as a weed-inhibiting mulch between plants and rows. When mixed with soil, it adds structure and absorbancy to allow air and water to reach the root system. Sawdust can be placed in the benches as a pot underlayer. Its water-retaining properties keep the pots wet longer and aid in root growth. *But* it is important to know what kind of sawdust you have. Hardwood sawdust can be used as-is. Sawdust made from pine and other soft-wooded trees may need to be mixed with a little lime to prevent it from souring your soil. Wood chips serve a similar purpose but, because of the size of the pieces, do not retain water as well nor will they compost down as rapidly. Observe the same precautions when using them. Both sawdust and wood chips will deplete soil nitrogen rapidly unless they are first aged for about a year. To be on the safe side, always fertilize with liquid fish emulsion or manure tea as soon as these mulches are in place.

If snails are a problem, cinders might help cut back on their migratory habits. In this day of oil–or gas–fired heat, cinders are scarce, but resurgence of the use of coal should make cinders available again.

Liquid fish emulsion, fish meal, blood meal, and manure teas round out the soil doctor's bag of tricks. All of these plant foods provide a smorgasbord of vitamins, minerals, and other nutrients and should be viewed as the apple a day that keeps the doctor at bay. Without them, plants are susceptible to disease, pest attacks, and general poor health. In this state plants are not good food for us, either. So, when you think about putting off the chore of fertilizing, think about what you are doing to yourself and I guarantee you'll be out in the greenhouse making amends in short order. The liquids should be added two to four times each month, depending on the amount of watering necessary and the speed of plant growth. Fish meal and blood meal should be incorporated into the soil during soil maintenance times in January and July.

COMPOST

We've mentioned compost a lot here and there in this book. Compost is the integral part of the growing medium that slowly releases food to the plants, heat to the soil, and carbon dioxide to the air. Compost plus good garden loam produces healthy, vigorous plants that reward us with bountiful harvests. I would be lost in my gardens without this commodity. But good compost doesn't grow on trees. It has to be made with a lot of help from Mother Nature.

There are about as many ways to make compost as there are organic gardeners—and then some. But all ways boil down to two basic techniques with a few variations.

The first method, anaerobic digestion, produces a rich organic fertilizer and methane gas. It takes place in the absence of oxygen and presents a few problems, the major one being odor. But you can get relatively fast digestion if anaerobic (airless) conditions are maintained and if temperatures are kept to about 95°F. For best results, the process should be carried out in an air-tight tank and the gases siphoned off as they are produced. One of two processes can be used—the batch process is just that. You mix up a batch of *slurry* (chopped organic materials or manure plus water) in the tank, warm it up, and then let 'er go. The continuous process allows you to feed slurry into the tank periodically while collecting gas and compost from the other end.

Aerobic digestion, the second method, is carried out in the presence of oxygen. The more oxygen in contact with the center of the pile, the faster the composting will be done. Aerobic composting can take anywhere from two weeks to a year to complete a batch. It takes a year if you just make a pile of organic materials and then do nothing to it. If you take that same pile and stir it up every two or three days, you can complete the process in two to three weeks.

For good results, you should pay attention to the types of organic material you place in your pile and to its basic carbon and nitrogen content. The best piles have a ratio of carbon to nitrogen of 30:1. You can get very scientific and try to figure all this out, or you can fly by the seat of your pants and probably do almost as well. The trick is to know that most fresh green materials will be higher in nitrogen, while wilted, brown materials and woody or tough stem plant parts will be higher in carbons. Animal wastes are high in nitrogen, as are seed, bone and blood meals and coffee grounds. If too much carbonaceous material is in the pile in proportion to nitrogen, the pile will not heat up because bacterial action is limited. If the amount of nitrogen is too high, a definite ammonia smell will pervade the air.

Your pile should combine manure with plant wastes— or mix in equal amounts of grass clippings and leaves. Tree prunings, chopped finely, are a good additive provided other materials are also used. Hay, spoiled by rain and unfit for animal food, is another resource if you live near farms. Urban dwellers can contact supermarkets or food processing plants for vegetable wastes. Those who may not find organic materials readily available should use imagination. Wherever organic wastes are generated, there is a source of supply.

The pile can be built right on the ground with no container. When it reaches a height of 3½ to 4 feet, start sloping the sides inward so the pile doesn't fall apart. Containers can be used. These range from specially constructed masonry bins to wooden frames or metal trash cans liberally punctured with

holes. However you build your container, be sure to leave air vents along the sides. The front panel should be removable so you have access to the pile for turning, and for removing the finished product.

Materials used in the pile should be shredded or chopped for best results. A rotary mower will chop up material as tough as old corn stalks if they are laid flat on the ground. All sorts of homebuilt rigs can do the job. *Organic Gardening Magazine* features these every so often. If you have no mechanized method, then invest in a machete or sharpen your hoe, spade, or mattock, and use elbow grease. The smaller the pieces, the faster your compost will be ready. Leaves are an especial nuisance because they tend to clump if not chopped finely.

Piles can be erected using the layer method or the mix method. In layers, a base composed of thin sticks and twigs or other coarse material is placed on the ground or the bottom of the container. A 9-inch layer of greens, leaves, etc., comes next. This is topped by a 3- to 4-inch layer of manure and capped by a sprinkling of garden soil or old compost. Repeat these last three layers until the pile is about 5 feet high. Add water to the pile until it feels moist. Cover with old rugs, plastic, bags, or other materials that will keep the rain out and retain the moisture in the pile.

The mix method, developed by Victor Dalpadado of Sri Lanka, is a way of taking the ingredients on hand (keeping in mind the carbon and nitrogen requirements), chopping them up, and mixing them in a pile. This, to me, seems to be very logical because it is difficult to have the right amounts of ingredients around to form layers all the time.

As in all things, there is a minimum size to the pile. The composting heap will not heat up efficiently if the pile is less than $3 \times 3 \times 3$ feet. Optimum size seems to be 5 feet square by 4 to 5 feet high. I've seen, and worked with, piles just 3 feet wide and as long as 5 or 6 feet. For me, anything higher than 4 feet is too high to work with comfortably. The factor that dictates the optimum size of the pile is the desired temperature of 160°F. At this temperature, many of the pathogenic disease vectors are killed, as are most weed seeds. In effect, the progress pasteurizes the compost.

Moisture is an important ingredient for the process of decomposition. There should be enough that, like a sponge, the pile has water in it, but not enough to shed when squeezed. The moisture can be added as the pile is built or upon completion. I prefer the former way because then I am sure that it is evenly distributed. Moisture can be water, manure tea, urine (a sterile body fluid successfully used by Dalpadado in place of manure), or other fluids such as nettle or comfrey teas.

Bacteria are another critical element to the functioning pile. Without them decomposition will not take place. To ensure the presence of bacteria in the pile, incorporate some garden loam or some old compost. I use about ten shovelsful for a $5 \times 5 \times 4$-foot pile. If conditions are not right, bacteria will not reproduce rapidly, so the digestive process will take a long time and will not produce as rich a product. The amount of nitrogen in the pile controls the rate at which they reproduce. The indicator that this is happening is the temperature, which should be 110° to 120°F by the end of the first twenty-four hours. After each turning, it should climb to 140° to 160°F, measured by a thermometer stuck into the center of the pile, over another twenty-four hours.

To maintain the high temperatures, and to keep the bacteria working, the pile should be turned every two to three days. When the temperature of the pile starts to drop, the oxygen supply is diminishing. When the temperature declines to 110°F or lower, and turning doesn't elevate it, the pile is done and can be used in the garden. It will probably have shrunk to one-half its original volume.

There is a technique to turning the pile that gives best results. First, turn the outer edges to form the center of a new pile; the center of the old pile should then form the outer edges of the new pile. This promotes a more even composting of the materials. Second, the material, as it is turned, should be chopped to eliminate lumps resulting from packing. This is vital if the materials used to build the pile were not shredded or finely chopped to begin with. If you have chickens, they will do a job on the outdoor pile. I have a hard time keeping our birds out of it long enough for it to heat up. They scatter the composting materials across the bin in their search for edibles.

The ways and means of composting are constantly changing and improving. Once you are attuned to this method of producing rich humus, you will want to keep up with the events in the field. I strongly recommend reading *Organic Gardening Magazine* put out by Rodale Press.

COMPOSTING IN THE GREENHOUSE

There are a number of excellent reasons for starting a composting bin in your greenhouse if you have the room. First, the composting process contributes heat to the greenhouse—several degrees of temperature at the peak of the process. Second, a by-product is the formation of carbon dioxide which stimulates plant growth. Third, greenhouse composting gives you additional humus for your cool weather gardening. It is handy to have in the cold months when the outside composters are inactive. (It is also handy to have a little extra soil on hand, for use when the ground outside is frozen.) Fourth, it does help to maintain higher humidity levels in the greenhouse.

My inside composter is an old trash can generously endowed with holes on all sides and in the bottom. It sits on two bricks and has a drop pan underneath to catch any liquids. Start the container with a 4-inch layer of loam and just keep adding chopped kitchen wastes, undiseased garden wastes, and every so often a shovelful of manure from another can. Watch the moisture level and, if the materials feel the least bit dry, spray the contents. To aerate the pile, jab it with a pitchfork every two days and try to stir it around a bit at the same time. When the can is about three-quarters full, stop adding material to it and just let it perk along, saving scraps in a covered can for the next pile. Depending on the amount of material I have for the pile, and how long it takes to build up, I will have compost in four to eight weeks by this method.

	SEED GERMINATION			TRANSPLANT SCHEDULE	
	Time (days)	Soil Temp. °F	Transplant Spacing	Timing	Comments
BEETS	4-10	60-70	2″ x 2″ in flats	2 months before average day-time temperature reaches 80°F	Soak seeds before sowing. 1 seed produces 4-5 plants. Immediately after seedlings appear, separate & transplant
BROCCOLI	10	60-70	2″ x 2″ in flats, or use peat pots	6 weeks before moving outside	Cold tolerant. Keep in flats, 6-packs, or peat pots until they are moved outside
BRUSSELS SPROUTS	10	60-70	2″ x 2″ in flats, or use peat pots	6 weeks before moving outside	Cold tolerant. Keep in flats, 6-packs, or peat pots until they are moved outside
CABBAGES	10	60-70	2″ x 2″ in flats, or use peat pots	6 weeks, until after adolescence	Can withstand frost & freeze but will not grow. Keep in flats, 6-packs, or peat pots until they are moved outside
CAULIFLOWER	10	60-70	2″ x 2″ in flats, or use peat pots	4-5 weeks	Sow in succession. Susceptible to temperature swings & adverse conditions when immature. Keep in flats, 6-packs, or peat pots
CELERY	10-20	60-70	3″ x 3″ in flats	10-12 weeks before transplanting outside	Keep seeds covered & moist. Germination is improved by raising & lowering temperature within 60-70°F range. Transplant outside only after night temperature stays above 55°F.
CHARD	6-10	50-85	2″ x 2″ in flats	3 weeks	
CORN	4-5	60-70	Do not transplant	4-5 weeks before ground temperature reaches 60°F	Plant in peat pots or 6-packs to start early where growing season is short
CUCUMBERS	5-6	65-75	Do not transplant	4-5 weeks before last expected frost	Grow only in peat pellets or peat pots; do not remove from pot. Needs lots of water, partial shade in hot weather. Plant outside 1 week after last frost
EGGPLANT	5-10	65-75	¼″ in peat pots	8 weeks before night temperature rises above 45°F average	Very cold-sensitive. Harden by reducing moisture
LEEKS		60-70	Sow 1″ apart; do not transplant	Sow in January for summer crop in northern latitudes	Sow directly into flats; these plants grow slowly at first. Move outside when you plant onions
OKRA	4-14	65-75	3″ x 3″ in flats or peat pots	8 weeks before outside soil temperature is expected to reach 65°F	Abrade seed before sowing. A warm-weather plant, so seedlings will allow growth in short-season areas

Table 3

52

	SEED GERMINATION			TRANSPLANT SCHEDULE	
	Time (days)	Soil Temp. °F	Transplant Spacing	Timing	Comments
ONIONS	6-10	60-70	Do not transplant indoors	8 weeks, or early January	Sow thinly in flats, pH 5.8-6.5; Seed-started onions are poor keepers
PEPPERS	6-14	65-75	Transplant to 3″ peat pots	10 weeks, or until night temperature is at least 55°F	Never let seedlings wilt; feed weekly with liquid fish emulsion. If outside planting time is cool, transplant to larger peat pots instead
SQUASH	4-7	65-75	Do not transplant	6 weeks before moving outside	Start seeds 2 per peat pot; when they sprout, snip off the weaker one
MUSKMELON CANTALOUPE WATERMELON	4-10	65-75	Do not transplant	4-5 weeks; move outside after night temperature reaches 55°F	Plant in peat pellets or pots, 2 seeds per pot. Snip off weaker plant. Cover with wisps of hay when first moved outdoors; mulch & water daily until established
TOMATOES	5-14	60-70	Transplant to 6-packs, then to peat pots	8 weeks before moving outside	Transplant when first true leaves appear, then 2 more times, planting deeper each time to increase root system; feed 1 week after transplant, then every 2-3 weeks. Use tepid water; do not overwater. Keep temperatures cool for strong plants
SWEET POTATOES	7-10	65-75	Transplant to peat pots	6 weeks before moving outside	Start by placing sweet potato half, cut side down, in soilless medium; keep moist; cover lightly with moist peat moss. When seedlings are 2″ high, carefully break from tuber, transplant to sandy, less fertile medium in peat pot

53

A P R I L

Strawberries under glass

The climate:
very active everywhere.
chores depend on the state of the plants,
which depend on the region
and the climate in the greenhouse

The chores:
continuing the care and
raising of seedlings;
planting trees (and bushes and vines)

*A*pril chores depend upon the status of your plants, which depends upon the climate in the greenhouse. The pull of the outdoors will be strong after the winter season, but this is also a very busy time in your greenhouse. You will be using your propagation box full tilt, germinating vegetable seeds and plants for your flower beds. There are times, in April, when I feel the movements in greenhouse and outside should be orchestrated to something like Ravel's *Bolero* or Khatchaturian's *Sabre Dance.* The only way to keep your sanity and assure accomplishment of all tasks on time is to keep April's calendar pinned to the wall, in plain sight. Check off finished tasks, plan ahead, and keep noting new jobs as they come to mind.

Fruit trees and plants, ordered in December, will arrive this month, and containers and soil mix will have to be ready and space available. Pot or plant immediately. If you cannot, place the trees in a bucket of water for a few days. If your schedule is such that it will be a week or more until you can plant them, heel them into some soil in a bucket and keep them moist.

My interest in growing fruits under glass was sparked when my neighbor, June Fuerderer, asked if I had ever tried raising grapes during the winter. She and I both grow strawberries—much to our satisfaction—but neither of us could find much information on other fruit.

Then I remembered those English novels where the family serves up fresh fruit from the greenhouse or conservatory in the dead of winter. So I went to Boston and the library of the Massachusetts Horticultural Society to see what they had on English cultivation of greenhouse fruits. Between the Society and the Boston Public Library, I found a wealth of materials published in the eighteenth and nineteenth centuries, and several modern treatises, also by English authors. The techniques have remained the same, although the varieties have changed.

Many fruits are easy to grow in most U.S. climates, but if you want to have fruit out-of-season, or fruit not suited to your climate, then greenhouses are your answer. I am just starting to grow fruits in my greenhouse. You may want to experiment and try your luck, so here is the information I have gleaned from old masters and modern fruit growers.

One word of caution. You can raise almost any cultivated fruit in the greenhouse under the right conditions, but you will want to exercise a little care in selecting fruit types for the solar greenhouse. The solar greenhouse grower is somewhat more in touch with the weather outside his greenhouse, and must either work with its effects on greenhouse climate or be willing to exert more control over the greenhouse climate. If your temperature swings are out of key with the needs of a particular fruit, you should consider not growing it. Fruits also require more attention at times than vegetables do, so make sure you have the time to give. And the soils used to grow fruit may be different from those used to grow vegetables.

In a small greenhouse, consider raising fruits in containers. They are transportable, and can be moved outside in warm weather or placed to take advantage of microclimates, allowing you to set each fruit in a very special place catering to specific needs. There are a few tricks to growing containerized fruit. They all relate to keeping the fruit trees or shrubs to manageable size so they can stay in containers. The first trick is to select a tree of the proper growth pattern, one that will stay small. Look for double dwarfs and miniature or bush varieties that can be pruned back. Some fruits, such as dwarf peach and

TRIMMING ROOTS

apple, must eventually be planted in the ground, however, as even dwarf stock does grow. Most vine and cane fruits such as strawberries and grapes, are pruned back every year and present few size problems.

The second trick is to pot and repot your tree or vine in the correct sizes of container, which naturally depends upon the size of the tree and the amount of root. Fruiting trees seem to do better in smaller containers than foliage trees. Cramping the roots stimulates fruit production.

It is important to pot correctly. First, fill the container one-third full of the 1–1–1 soil mix (or other mix as prescribed for the plant). Place the tree on this and fan the roots out over the soil. Hold the tree erect in the center of the pot and steady it—the tree must not shift during the potting process. Gradually add more soil. Carefully work the soil between the roots, pressing it down as you go, until you are within 1 to 2 inches of the top of the pot. The amount of room left depends upon the pot size: the bigger the pot, the more room left. If necessary, stake the tree or vine. When repotting your tree (usually done in January or February), trim the roots about one-third. This helps to maintain the dwarf characteristic. You may be able to use the same pot for several years before the plant will no longer fit in it. Also, you should carefully keep the top foliage trimmed back. Pruning techniques are established by the type of tree. If you are growing orchard fruits in your greenhouse, consult the references in December for information on pruning.

Fruit trees should be fed yearly. Part of this feeding process is to repot the trees or to renew at least one-third of the soil in the container each year. After the third year, mulch with well-rotted compost. Before adding the compost mulch, you can scratch 1 teaspoon of blood meal into the top inch of soil. If the tree does not do well on this diet, use the dilute liquid fish emulsion every two weeks until you notice improvement. Trees that are overfed run to foliage rather than fruit.

In order to produce good fruits, you will have to thin heartlessly, especially during the first few years. Each year you can increase the number of fruits you allow to remain. At the end of the fourth *bearing* year, you should harvest about two dozen fruits from each pear, peach, or nectarine tree. For apricot and plum trees, thin a quarter to a third of the fruit the first year, a sixth the second year, and none the third year or after.

You will gradually have to increase the size of the containers. Once a tree outgrows the half-barrel size, you should consider planting it outside. You will have enjoyed a number of years of fine fruit from your indoor tree and, if it is a fruit that grows naturally in your climate, you can continue to collect bountiful harvests in season after it has been permanently located outside. Miniatures and some of the dwarfs that retain their small size should give you years of good picking from your greenhouse orchard.

The English grow much of their high quality fruit in orchard houses—glass houses designed for indoor fruit production. These are constructed like greenhouses but they are a little taller. The fruit trees or vines are planted along the south wall and trained to grow up trellises placed 6 to 8 inches below the glass. The trees are pruned by espalier techniques so that maximum sunlight can penetrate throughout the tree.

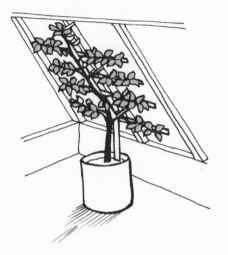

GROWING FRUIT AGAINST THE GLASS

BERRIES

In New England, blueberries are so prolific in the wild state and the berries freeze so nicely that I wouldn't plant a blueberry bush inside or out. But many people don't have the same choice. **Blueberries** are easy to raise if you remember to keep the soil very acid pH 4 to 5. To do this, mix copious amounts of oak leaf or pine needle compost with sawdust and a heavy, clayey soil, in a ratio of one to one. To provide good drainage, place some broken pottery in the bottom of the container. Blueberries like lots of moisture but not a soggy, wet soil. They grow wild on the tufty ground near bogs but not where they are immersed in water. Commercial varieties ripen at different times, so select several bushes to spread the harvest season over a long period of time. Never prune except to remove dead wood or weak shoots. In greenhouses blueberries can grow two crops each year, if you leave them outside until December or January. They are frost hardy, but be sure to protect the root system in the pot from freezing. Then, when you bring them in, you can have spring and late summer harvests. Feed them regularly with liquid fish emulsion. If the leaves turn yellow, it is a symptom of iron deficiency caused by sweet soil. Check soil pH and readjust accordingly with aluminum sulfate.

Currants and gooseberries: These related fruits should not be grown within 900 feet of White Pines. They are a vector in transmitting White Pine Blister Rust. For this reason, it is illegal to ship them into some states. Check with your state agricultural extension agent before purchasing stock.

Purchase potted stock and leave it outdoors until mid-December. Make sure the potting soil is always moist; they thrive on quite damp soil. Before bringing the plants indoors, prune off all weak, non-bearing shoots. Cuttings for new plants can be taken at this time and stored in a dark place in moist peat moss for propagation in the spring. The foliage should be misted during the hot months and periodically during the rest of the year to reduce the likelihood of pest infestation. If you keep these plants in your greenhouse during the summer, place them in a shady, well-ventilated spot.

Strawberries are not difficult to grow in the greenhouse, but you must work with the strawberry scheme of things. They can be raised from seed or runners.

One type, the alpine varieties that taste much like the wild strawberries we gather in our fields every July, can be grown from seed available through most seed houses. Start the seeds in early spring for a fall–winter crop. Sow in a soilless mix, and as soon as the young plants can be handled, transfer them to containers with a rich, humusy soil mix. These berries are everbearing, so you can expect to get light crops all through the summer and a heavier one in the fall. To strengthen the plant, however, most of the blossoms should be picked off the first part of the season. By autumn, each plant will have produced two or three crowns that can be separated to increase the number of plants.

STRAWBERRY RUNNERS

Alpine varieties have not yet been bred for resistance to the strawberry diseases. It is best to replace your stock every two years to prevent a build–up of disease organisms and viruses. I bring two dozen new runners into the greenhouse in the fall after the weather has consistently been below 10°F at night for three to four weeks. To do this, in the spring I plant clay pots along my outdoor strawberry rows. As the runners form, I pin them to the ground with wire "hairpins" to train them to grow in these pots. In the fall, most of these new plants are then moved to new outdoor beds, and some are brought into the greenhouse for the new crop. There should be two plants in each 10-inch pot or three plants in each 12-inch pot.

Use the standard 1–1–1 soil mix with extra compost and a little lime in the pots. Strawberries are heavy feeders. To save space in the greenhouse, I grow this fruit in a tower arrangement of shelves that allows me to stack the pots, two to a shelf. The shelves do not allow water to drip from above onto plants below. A sheet of heavy-duty freezer weight aluminum foil placed on top of the shelves does the trick. Used aluminum printing plates, shaped into trays will also do it (four for $1 at our local newspaper).

Now comes the tricky part for solar greenhouse growers: Strawberries' flowering process is initiated by short days first—but long days are needed to stimulate bud formation and flower stalk elongation. The short/long day need is overridden if the temperature can be kept at about 55°F for two weeks. Then, if the temperature is elevated to 65°F, the buds will form and stalks will grow.

Strawberries will have to be hand pollinated.

It is important to keep strawberry plants moist until after fruit sets. Humid conditions favor pollination. After fruit sets, water weekly with a weak (½ teaspoon liquid fish emulsion to 1 gallon water) fertilizer. Be sure to ventilate if the sun is out and temperatures are over 70°F, especially when fruit is forming and ripening.

Strawberries also can be grown under lights. In the fall, take the runners you have potted and place them in a protected outside area, mulching around them to prevent frost kill.

In January, bring them inside and place them 5 feet from a hanging filament lamp (200 watts) for eight hours each night. This speeds growth up by about two weeks. Temperatures should be in the 60°F day to 50°F night range.

Strawberries are susceptible both to verticulum wilt and to Red Stele disease. Strains resistant to these diseases can be purchased. The plants can be infected if grown in beds where such crops as tomatoes and peppers grew, so keep them in containers to prevent disease.

CITRUS FRUITS

Californians may not want to take up valuable space growing citrus fruits but, to me, a lemon tree in mid-winter looks and smells mighty nice. Many nurseries now have dwarf varieties suitable for growing indoors and in any greenhouse where night temperatures can be kept above 45° to 50°F.

Citruses, especially oranges, do require well-defined summer and winter seasons and moderate amounts of water. They can develop considerable tolerance to cool weather, but they will not bear ripe fruit where temperatures are too low. Fruit flavor and size are best when grown at a *mean* temperature of 65°F. General ranges: in the spring, 50°F rising to 70°F by May; mid-summer temperatures not above 85°F. Citrus requires maximum light, but must be shaded lightly in strong sunlight.

Oranges may be propagated by inserting 5-inch shoots into pots of sandy soil kept at 70° to 75°F in a propagating frame. Or, layer suitable branches into pots filled with well–drained potting mix.

Layering is a way to propagate plants that are difficult to reproduce in any other way. The most common and easiest technique, of several, is the air layering method. Select a stem that is vigorous and healthy but not overly old. Remove the bark from about one-third of the circumference of the stem a few inches below the leaves. Take a handful of moist peat moss and pack it around the stripped area. Tie a clear piece of plastic over this so that it is water-tight. After six to eight

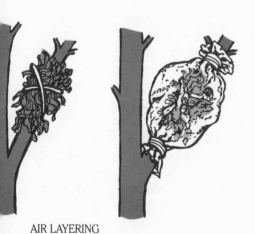

AIR LAYERING

GROUND LAYERING

weeks, when you can see the rootlets emerging through the peat moss, remove the plastic, separate the rooted stem from the parent plant, and pot it.

To ground layer, scrape the stem and bend it down to a pot filled with growing medium. Bury the scraped area about 2 inches deep in the pot. Keep the soil moist at all times. The major disadvantage of this form of layering is that the only way to tell when an adequate root system has formed on the stem is to dig it up carefully.

Fruit stock is usually grafted: a piece of one tree is attached to a piece of another tree. There are a number of ways to graft, depending upon the stock and condition under which the tree is growing. Check a book on grafting fruit trees for the method best suited to your project. (Some apples may be grafted as many as four times: once for sturdy root stock, once or twice for dwarfing characteristics, and one or more times for fruit. Each graft contributes to the overall characteristics of the tree and its produce.) In all cases, grafted stock will be hardier, and can be resistant to some diseases (check this before buying a tree). It will produce better fruit than trees raised from seeds of citrus fruit bought in the supermarket.

The soil used for potting mix is adequate for citrus fruits with the addition of bone meal, 12 cups to a bushel of soil mix. Top-dress the plant with rotted manure compost annually. When potting or repotting, use the smallest pot that will hold the root system—an 11-inch pot should be adequate for a three-year-old plant. Water the plant until water runs out of the drainage holes. Periodically mist the foliage to simulate rainfall, and keep the surrounding greenhouse floor damp. This is especially important during the warm season. After the scion (twig grafted to root shoot) buds have started to grow, remove all the lower shoots. Pruning should be done only in winter, and the wounds should be painted over. During the first two years, water sprouts may form on the upper sides of the branchlets. These may be cut back to the origin if it is necessary to keep a symmetrical tree. However, they develop into fruiting wood, so don't prune harshly. Do prune the center of the tree to allow light to enter and to promote air circulation.

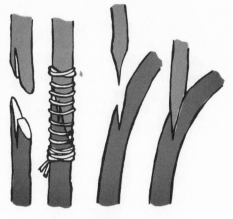

GRAFTING

Do not prune after buds have opened in the spring except to remove dead wood and to assure that the branches do not become overcrowded in the center of the plant.

The soil should be kept moist at all times during the growing season. Cut back to monthly waterings during dormancy. Provide full ventilation during the warm months to prevent mildews. Most blossoms will form in the spring. They are usually self-pollinating, but it will not hurt to give the limbs a gentle shake daily. It takes nine to twelve months for fruit to ripen.

Common diseases are generally related to poor cultivation techniques such as overwatering, poorly drained soil, or exposure to frost. Most of the pests thrive naturally in citrus-growing areas. These include mites, scale, mealy bugs, whitefly, and nematodes specifically adapted to feeding from citrus trees.

Some nice miniature and dwarf citruses fruit prolifically and are attuned to producing year-round indoors. *Citrus mitis* (miniature orange) produces a constant supply of 1 to 1½ inch oranges (eat them skin and all). Like many citruses, it will produce blossoms and ripening fruit concurrently. It is a hardy tree and the most cold-tolerant orange. If your greenhouse is tall, you might consider growing a standard variety.

Mandarin, a separate citrus species similar in cultivation to the orange, can be grown in the greenhouse. It becomes cold–resistant when the mean temperature falls below 60 °F and will winter over in temperatures down to 45 °F. Early in spring, gradually raise the daily mean temperature (average of day and night temperature) to 60 °F to stimulate growth. Maximum temperatures should reach 85 °F by midsummer. Fruit should be ready by late December. *Satsuma* and *Clementine* varieties are small.

Lemons do not require as high temperatures to set fruit as oranges do, but are not as cold–tolerant either. They will stop setting fruit and become dormant after several days and nights of near–freezing temperatures. Winter minimums are: 45 °F days and 40°F nights. With maximum light and warm temperatures they will produce fruit year-round, especially if they are receiving adequate moisture. They are ideal winter house and summer patio plants. Do not prune lemon trees except to remove dead wood and overcrowding branches during the winter months. Cultivation is similar to that of the orange. Lemons are especially susceptible to Leaf Scab, which can be promoted by overwatering. Watch for corky lesions on leaves and shoots.

Three varieties are commonly available, and others can be obtained by contacting nurseries specializing in these fruits. Ponderosa lemons, as their name implies, are large—equal to three normal-size lemons. As they may weigh 1 to 1½ pounds, be sure to prop up bearing branches. *Meyer,* or Chinese, lemon bears normal-size lemons in goodly quantities. This variety is sturdy and the most resistant to cold, but is susceptible to some of the citrus viruses. *Eureka,* a perennial bearer under optimum conditions, grows a high quality seedless fruit on a small tree.

Limes should be treated much like lemons, but are even more sensitive to cold temperatures. Their fruit is inclined to be very acid. Dwarf varieties can produce a high quality, juicy fruit on small vigorous trees. Try the *Mexican Bar* and *Persian varieties.*

Citrus fruits store best on the tree. If you maintain healthy growing conditions, fruit can be left as long as six months.

GRAPES

Viticulture has always been of interest to me. I enjoy making wine, and fresh grapes are, to me, one of the nicest fruits available. The New Hampshire winter climate is too severe for all but the hardiest varieties outdoors, so I am starting to grow some of my favorites under glass.

Grapes require potash for good growth. To four parts of the standard 1–1–1 greenhouse soil mix, add one part wood ash, or two parts granite dust or greensand. Each year, either in October or January depending on when you start to prepare for the next crop, top-dress the plant. Remove the top 2 to 3 inches of soil and bury this in the compost pile outdoors—it is still rich in organic material. Sprinkle a mixture of fertilizer on top of the exposed soil around the vine and prick it into the soil with a fork. Top-dress with a 3–1–1 mix of loam, rotted manure, and wood ash (or other source of potassium). Dust the dressing lightly with lime and a little bone meal. Soak the plant with 2 to 3 gallons of water.

Grapes grown outside, and in greenhouses where there is room, are often trellised laterally. However, there are other ways they can be supported. The Guyot system, developed by Dr. Guyot, is described here. First, insert an 8 to 10 foot rod, bamboo, or pipe either into the pot or into the ground directly behind the pot. A second rod can be tied horizontally to the first at a spot about 2 feet above the pot. The leader is trained up the main cane until it reaches about 1 foot from the top. Pinch the growing point. While the leader is growing, all lateral

GUYOT TRELLIS

growth except for two short, three-budded spurs should be cut off with a sharp knife. Never use scissors or secateurs to cut a grape vine. A lateral spur is allowed to grow along each side of the cane. Short vertical stems of one to three leaves are allowed to grow along the leader and lateral spurs. After harvest, prune the vine to leave the best three canes for next year's growth. Old canes should be cut back to the main stem. Remove any non-bearing canes as fruit ripens, so all energies are directed to maturing the fruit. Depending on the age of the purchased stock, it may take two to three years to obtain the first harvest. Grape vines take about four years to mature.

Grape leaves need maximum sunlight, good ventilation, and high humidity until the first flowers open. Humidity can be maintained by wetting floors twice daily and by misting the leaves first thing in the morning. Grapes are prone to mildew diseases, so the misting is important to wash fungus spores from the leaves. Most grapes like a cool temperature—45° to 50°F at night, rising to 55°F when flowering. Be sure to ventilate to prevent scalding by high day temperatures and to keep the cooler climate required. Once the flowers have set, avoid wetting the foliage and overwetting the soil. Keep the plant adequately watered but a little on the dry side. As the grapes form, they should be thinned to allow air circulation through the bunch. Remove one-eighth to one-half of the grapes on each bunch so that a pencil can pass around each grape. This should result in larger grapes and few with mildew.

After you have harvested your crop, fully ventilate to stimulate leaf fall.

When selecting grape varieties, consider your greenhouse climate carefully. Most grapes do not do well in hot climates; you might be able to grow a cool–weather grape in a winter greenhouse. If you have a warm greenhouse, your plants will need more food than those in a cool climate. Late varieties take six months to mature, while earlier varieties require just five months.

FIGS AND OTHER FRUITS

Figs are an excellent fruit crop for any greenhouse where the temperature does not drop below freezing. They are best grown in pots, because confining the root system promotes fruit production. The plants will grow well in the standard 1–1–1 greenhouse growing medium to which a little bone meal has been added. A slightly alkaline soil will keep the plant small and produce quality fruit.

Stock can be purchased or raised from cuttings propagated in sand. Cuttings are taken in late fall from the short, jointed shoots of the previous year's growth. They should be 8 to 12 inches long with 1 inch of older wood at the base of the cutting. Insert the cutting 6 inches into the rooting medium and cover it with peat moss, straw, or leaves. Lift and pot it the following autumn in 4–inch pots. After the root mass fills these pots, transfer to 10 to 12–inch pots. For best results, repot the tree each year into the same–size pot, trimming the root system a little on repotting.

Prune in two ways. When potting the first time, cut the tree back to 18 inches. This promotes development of an open bush. To keep a compact, well–shaped head, the tree should thereafter be pruned in March and in the following months to keep young shoots from overcrowding. These shoots are your bearing stock, so be careful not to prune away too much. Lateral shoots should be cut at the sixth leaf, after the leaves fall in the autumn.

Figs can stand temperatures to 10°F when dormant, but can be severely harmed by temperatures lower than 30°F when growing in the spring. In the warm greenhouse, figs can produce two to three crops each year. The first, in early summer, will be on last year's wood; the second, in the fall, will be on new wood. To achieve this, your tree must receive maximum sunlight and temperatures starting at 65°F, raised slowly to 80°F.

If growth slows or stops, add a nitrogen fertilizer such as dilute liquid fish emulsion. Be sure to keep soil moist until fruits start to ripen. At this time, reduce water to prevent cracked fruit. Humidity should be kept high by watering the floors and ventilating. To have high quality fruit, grow no more than three on each shoot.

There are four types of figs. Three—the *Smyrna,* white *San Pedro,* and *Caprifig*—require pollination by a tiny wasp *(Blastophaga)* that grows only in warm climates, or by an artificial hormone spray. Adriatic varieties are self–pollinating, and are the only ones grown in cooler climates. If you have a cool greenhouse, hardy standard Adriatic varieties include *White Marseilles, White Ischia,* and *White Genoa. Mission, Negro Largo,* and *Brown Turkey* (Magnolia) are tolerant to warmer temperatures and should be only grown outside.

Ficus carica is an excellent dwarf for greenhouse culture, the only dwarf to produce edible fruit. It does not require artificial pollination or the pruning necessary to maintain a small size in other varieties.

Melons like a soil temperature that hovers between 70° and 75°F. They do not like too acid a soil, or large quantities of fertilizer. However, if you can prepare a hot bed in your greenhouse, or can slip a heating coil under a large container, try growing some of these fruits. Varieties such as *New Hampshire Granite,* and *Minnesota Midget* have short growing seasons and are small melons. The Japanese melon varieties are also very sweet and will hang tenaciously onto the vine until fully ripe.

Start two seedlings in each 2½–inch peat pot, for twice the number of plants you need. Germinate at 75°F soil temperature. When the seedlings are about 2 inches high, snip off the weaker plant. If you grow melons in containers, use large pots—on the order of a bushel basket or half-barrel. Fill with the 1–1–1 mix to which has been added bone meal, lime, and, if possible, one shovelful of charcoal. Place two seedlings in each large container, about 8 inches apart. Keep the seedlings in full sun and do not let the temperature dip below 60°F at night. When the daytime temperature reaches 70°F, vent. Many melon varieties will require hand–pollination. Do this in the morning, using a soft brush or gently shaking the vines.

HAND POLLINATING

Pinch off all non–fruiting side shoots. If the fruit is large, support it in a mesh bag made of cheesecloth or old stockings.

Melons are susceptible to mildews, so the foliage should be misted about once a week to wash off fungus spores. Otherwise, avoid wetting the leaves. Keep floors dampened in dry, hot weather to keep humidity levels high.

The English sometimes grow their melons on decomposed straw bales. To do it, loosen up a bale, and add dilute liquid ammonium sulphate all winter to keep the straw moist. Decomposition will be well–progressed by spring, in time to plant an early crop.

You can force **rhubarb** to produce an early crop in the greenhouse. Before the ground freezes in the fall, dig up some roots and place them in a bushel basket full of moistened soil mix. Wrap in plastic and put in a cold garage, storage shed, or protected outdoor area. Rhubarb must have at least two weeks of night temperatures below 10°F to grow. If your temperatures drop lower than this, be prepared to mulch with hay, dead leaves, or another form of protection. Once the roots have endured the cold conditions they could be brought into a cool greenhouse. When you are ready to force them, fill a large container (half–bushel minimum) with the 1–1–1 soil mix to within 4 inches of the top. Place the clump in the container with the roots fanned out. Carefully work in 3 inches of the soil mix to fill all the nooks and crannies around the root system. Keep the soil moist rather than wet. Optimum temperatures are: 60°F days and 50°F minimum at night.

A word of caution: the *LEAVES OF RHUBARB ARE POISONOUS.* Eat only the stems.

OUTDOOR FRUITS FOR INDOORS

For those who cannot grow fruit except under glass, here are a few fruits not traditionally grown in greenhouses, with varieties particularly adaptable to containerized growing:

Nectarines and **peaches** have both been miniaturized for container gardening. Nectarina (Nectarine) and Bonanza peach stocks are available from Stark Nurseries and several other nurseries specializing in fruit trees. They prefer warm, sunny locations and sandy soil. If the trees grow too rapidly, reduce the amount of food you give them. They require stringent pruning to produce good fruits.

Most **pear** trees require other pear trees for pollination. The Duchess variety is self-pollinating and produces large fruits. It is especially important to thin out the fruits for the first three years or the weight of the fruit will break the branches.

If you like **plums,** consider raising the dwarf Damson for plum preserves or one of the other dwarfs that produce eating plums. Some of the Damsons are self-pollinating, but most plums require at least one other plum *of the right family* for pollination. When selecting a plum variety, be sure also to select another variety recommended as a pollinator. Plums require regular feeding. Keep the soil moist, not wet, and mist the foliage when watering during the growing season. Plums are susceptible to black knot (limbs) and brown rot (tree and fruit). Black knot can be controlled by pruning out all infected parts. Native hybrid stocks tend to be resistant. Brown rot, however, just leaves you with a mess of bad fruit. Sanitation is the main control.

Dwarf **apricots** adapt nicely to containerized gardening. While most are self–pollinating, they will produce more fruit if two different varieties are grown. Fruit must be stringently thinned for best results.

These fruits all grow well in soil composed of two parts garden loam and one part compost. The peach likes a sandier soil, so include one part of sand for this tree. Make sure your container has adequate drainage holes. The English seem to have great luck if they cover the drainage openings with a few lumps of charcoal.

VARIETIES FOR THE NORTH AMERICAN GREENHOUSE	
Cool climates	**Color**
Early Giant	Bluish black, excellent quality
Campbells Early	Bluish black, excellent quality
Ontario	White, small to medium berry, exceptional
Fredonia Early	Black, vigorous producer, good flavor
Schuyler	Black, medium berry, excellent hybrid
Concord	Black, medium grape; distinctive taste, multipurpose; vigorous and hardy
Warden	Sweeter than the Concord
Seneca	White, very large grape, excellent taste
Agawam	Purple black; medium size; "foxy" taste
Delaware	Red; medium large size; very sweet
Sheridan	Blue; medium size; excellent
Interlaken Early	Golden; seedless; very sweet. High quality. Hardy to −20°F
Warm Climates	
Pearl of Csaba	White; for the Northwest
Delight	Golden seedless of good quality
Thompson Seedless	Fine for hot California valleys and interior Oregon and Washington valleys.
Ribier	Black grape of excellent quality
Scarlet	Black with sweet, good flavor; vigorous.
White Muscat of Alexandria	Golden grape with very sweet flavor
Niagara Midseason	White; similar to Concord but sweeter

Many European grape varieties are of interest also. They have a broad range of flavors and colors. Select varieties specifically appropriate to your tastes and needs.

Table 4

M A Y

Getting Tough; Moving Out.

The climate:
warm everywhere.
a tug of war between inside and
outside gardens

The chores:
getting the seedlings out
getting heat-loving plants in

The last of the seedlings for the vegetable garden will be started shortly after the first of this month, in the northernmost places.

Many of those sprouted earlier move out to the cold frame to harden up before being planted in the garden. All of your energies are directed towards the outside world. You have the food garden to care for and all your flower bedding plants to put out. All in all, another busy month!

While you garden outside, give some thought to your warming greenhouse, a special climate to provide shelter for plants you might not otherwise be able to grow in your location. You may want to bring some of your house plants into the greenhouse for a change of scenery, or you may try growing herbs. They like a warm, sunny climate and, if yours is inclined to be cool at night outdoors, the greenhouse might be the best place for those little gardens.

The warm weather greenhouse garden grows when days are long but not necessarily sunny, and average daily temperatures range from 60° to 90°F. It grows luxuriously if maintained on proper amounts of food and water. *Depending on location and climate,* seedlings for this garden can be started sometime between the middle of winter and midspring, and the garden is producing between the vernal equinox (March 21) and mid-October. Heat-tolerant plants do well in this garden.

73

In this climate you might try such items as sweet potatoes in a barrel, or a small tropical fruit tree. But there's no sense in being overrun each winter by an avocado orchard or a ceiling-scraping papaya, because you must be prepared to take any warmth-loving perennials into the house as soon as the temperatures drop below 60°F. Keep your warm weather greenhouse garden containerized so it can be moved easily from sun to shade and even outside on very nice days.

I worked in a conventional glasshouse once where the heat was so intense that one of us was employed to hose the rest of the crew down every half hour. So I was pleasantly surprised the first summer we had our solar greenhouse. With all the vents open, the natural breezes kept it at the same temperature as outside. Only during still days did we have to turn on the fans. Most people assume that plants can take lots of heat. This is false. Many warmth-loving plants do well at temperatures between 65° and 90°F, but by the time temperatures have reached 95°F, growth stops in all but the hardiest, most heat-resistant varieties. Plants can't jump in the swimming pool or take a shower to cool off. They die at temperatures above 120° to 130°F. They are dependent on nature or the humans caring for them; therefore you must be in tune with the weather, and prepared to take action if your greenhouse is in danger of overheating. Once a plant has wilted or endured excessive temperatures for more than a short time, it is, in effect, handicapped for life.

Vents must be open day and night during the summer to allow natural cooling cycles to work properly. Increasing the humidity of the greenhouse can also have a cooling effect because a fair amount of heat is expended to evaporate water—although spraying the floors and walls of your greenhouse several times each day does pose problems for plants that do not like an excess of humidity. I have found it easiest to plan a garden to be raised either in dry conditions or in humid. In a small greenhouse it is hard to grow both.

Many fungus and rot diseases like the warm, moist weather of the greenhouse in summer and will flourish if you are not careful. Keep dead leaves and flowers picked, mist

foliage weekly or more often if warranted, and inspect the plants for signs of disease daily; immediately remove any diseased parts. During the day, have one or more small (1/20th horsepower) fans stirring the air in your greenhouse enough to circulate air around the leaves and stems of the plants. With ventilation, this will decrease disease risks.

Plants grow vigorously in this warm climate, and should be fed weekly except where noted. Use dilute-solution (1 tablespoon to 1 gallon) liquid fish emulsion, or manure tea, for this job. If fruiting plants are growing only foliage, cut back to feeding every other week, or less frequently.

Microclimates are very important to the growth of your plants in this warm greenhouse. Look for the cooler spots. Herbs that are not fussy about sunshine grow well toward the back of the greenhouse in the shade, if they receive good light reflected from the back wall. The best locations combine cool temperatures with long day length. Sunlight need not be bright—a few hours sun per day is enough for good growth, and will not burn the leaves. Move the plants to match the sun's path along the bed. This also gives room to start working new loam and compost into the ground bed in preparation for the cool greenhouse.

The big secret to summer greenhouse gardening is, as usual, to know the environment in which you will be working. If outdoor temperatures rocket into the 90°s regularly, and the air tends to be humid, your greenhouse will, at the very least, have these same characteristics. My greenhouse, on a breezy day, has the same temperature and humidity conditions as are found outside, but on a still day temperatures can climb 10° and 20°F higher than outside. Fans and watering help immensely, but may not be enough. Natural shading of the south wall keeps temperatures on the cool side with less work and is more reliable.

My first summer greenhouse garden consisted of herbs. These plants like dry, warm, light locations and lend themselves to experimentation because most are very hardy. Most herbs used in cooking originated in the Mediterranean region and are accustomed to that kind of climate. That summer, I was able to raise herbs that had previously defied all my attempts outside. I was able to control the heat by dampening floors twice a day, and still to keep a relatively dry environment by venting day and night. We had our usual August heat wave with temperatures in the high 90°s, when I moved the plants to the back of the greenhouse, over the water barrels where maximum venting occurred.

Many fruits like warm, sunny sheltered locations. Our nights outside are cool, so the greenhouse seems to be the ideal summer location for those that cannot tolerate much coolness. The citruses do well here, as do miniature peaches and nectarines.

Our vegetable garden has expanded to include some crops that do not normally do well in our climate. Eggplant and collard greens, to mention two, are easily raised in the ground bed. Sweet potatoes occupy a couple of battered trash cans placed along the south wall. And, for next year, we are contemplating trying to raise a few okra plants.

We have been having poor luck with tomatoes and peppers outside, lately. According to some learned weather sources, our climate is cooling and we are going to have to get used to shorter growing seasons; in some areas, it is already two weeks shorter than it was back in the 1940s. So I plan to experiment with a few plants of several tomato varieties this coming year to see how they behave. If the experiment works, I may grow more tomatoes under cover.

Lots of plants will do poorly in the warm greenhouse. Peas, members of the onion family, lettuces, radishes, and the brassicas all prefer cool weather. In fact, all the vegetable varieties that are prime candidates for the greenhouse in cool weather should be avoided in the summer greenhouse. Instead, search seed catalogs for heat-tolerant varieties. This, however, does not mean that you cannot sprout seedlings for the cool-weather greenhouse garden (see July). Sprout them, then move them outside to your cold frame area. Protect them from excessive heat and sunshine until they have vigorous growth. After they are strong, they can be taken to the garden or left in the cold frame until it is time to bring them inside in September.

Keeping in mind the limitations of the warm weather greenhouse, you should feel free to experiment. There are two rules to remember: First, water your plants daily in the morning. Always check the soil before watering to make sure the plant needs it. Plants in small pots may have to be watered twice a day because their reserves of water will not carry them for twenty-four hours. Don't water on cloudy days if the soil is still moist. Mist foliage once or twice each week. Second: Feed your plants weekly unless cultivation techniques specify otherwise. Watch the foliage. If it turns yellow or becomes mottled, find out what is missing in the plant's diet (See "Soils For the Solar Greenhouse," page 39.) If foliage is luxuriant and fruit is scarce, reduce the feeding schedule to once every two weeks. Treat the plants as individuals with specific dietary needs.

MOVING OUT

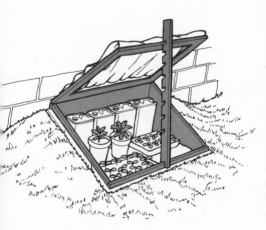

Seedlings raised for the outdoor garden should go out after all danger of frost has passed. If you start your seedlings too early, they will be too far advanced for the garden. Transplanting is a great shock to a plant also putting its energy into blooming. The chart on page 52 tells you how many weeks are required to produce plants to the right stage. To have seedlings that are vigorous yet adolescent, find out when your last frost date will be and count back. For example, if your last frost date is on June 9th, as ours is, and it takes six weeks to grow the broccoli seedlings, start germinating the seeds by the end of April.

You cannot expect seedlings that have been coddled, that have led a sheltered existence, to take readily to being shoved out into the cold, cruel world. All plants are susceptible to the shocks associated with temperatures cooler than they are used to, and the drying effects of the wind. The process of hardening off allows the plant to become acclimated to its new environment gradually, and encourages healthy, vigorous growth to meet this new challenge. Think of this as similar to acclimating yourself to a spring-fed lake after lying on the beach in the sun. Gradually wading into the water gives you time to adjust; taking the plunge can be brutal.

Hardening off can be done almost anywhere outside as long as the place is somewhat sheltered from the wind and provides good sunshine on most days. We have used a south-facing porch, rock shelters, and cold frames. Each of these areas provided good growing conditions during the day and could be covered to protect the plants from the night cold. The rock shelter worked well, because the heat stored in the rocks during the day helped to warm the plants at night. Now I always include a few big rocks or some bricks in my cold frames.

We make our cold frames out of 1×12-inch lumber that is cut to slope slightly toward the south. The size of the frame is determined by the size of the covering. Generally, coverings are recycled wooden storm windows but we have also made sashes and wrapped them with builder's-weight clear plastic. We keep an assortment of sticks next to the frames to prop the sash up for venting. Against cool weather, we usually place 2 inches of Styrofoam along the outside of each board, or berm the frame with earth or hay bales.

A 2-inch

layer of hay is laid inside the box and the plants are placed on this.

The cold frame built for the tomatoes is somewhat different in that the tomato plants are transplanted to a soil bed in the frame. The soil is worked to a depth of 12 inches and includes a goodly amount of compost. The tomatoes are spaced 4 inches apart in the bed and dug in deep enough to cover several inches of stem. This stimulates strong root growth and will make a plant better able to withstand dry weather. Aged sawdust is mulched around the plants. The tomato cold frame is twice as high as the other frames: 24 inches along the back, 18 inches in front, and the sides tapering down from back to front.

Our cold frames are located along the south-facing wall just below the greenhouse vents. A lilac bush provides some shade during the hottest part of the day, and prevailing winds keep air circulating. Having the cold frames in this location makes the hardening-off process a part of the natural move outward in spring and inward in the fall.

Check the plants in the cold frame as carefully as you tend to your gardens elsewhere. These plants require daily watering and weekly feeding unless otherwise specified. Tomatoes growing in a bed should not be fed, nor will they require as much water as seedlings growing in pots and flats. Their roots have greater access to nutrients and water.

Keep coverings handy to throw over the glass during the night if the temperatures are to fall below 40°F. Cold temperatures slow growth and in some crops will cause poor fruiting. Always be aware of the temperature outside. When your cold frame reaches 70°F vent it a little. As the day warms up, you may have to vent more. Then, as the cool evening approaches, you will gradually have to close the glass.

GROWING EGGPLANT, CUCUMBERS, AND PEPPERS IN THE WARM WEATHER GREENHOUSE

These are excellent candidates for the container garden in the warm weather greenhouse.

Cucumbers like warm soil temperatures, high humidity, and a good supply of water. When these conditions are optimal, and there are ten to twelve hours of light each day, plant some cucumber seeds in peat pots, two seeds per 2½ inch -diameter pot. The seeds will germinate in about seven days at soil temperatures of 70°F. After three weeks, snip off the weaker seedling in each pot and place the seedling, still in the peat pot, in a container large enough for a permanent home. The vines need support, so include trellising materials in the pot at this time. Bush varieties are available.

Most cucumbers produce a large number of male flowers, which will drop off. The females, which have tiny cucumbers just behind the flowers, will have to be hand-pollinated with a small brush. To assure a long and goodly harvest, keep soil temperatures above 60°F and pick the cukes when they are 6 to 7 inches long. If the fruit reaches maturity, the plant will feel it has done its job of providing for the next generation, and will cease flowering.

Mist the leaves at least once each week to keep down mildews. Misting is also important on very hot days: it keeps the plant cool.

Cucumbers like a rich soil to start, and should be fed frequently to keep them in good health.

Eggplants will take all the warmth you can give them, and then some. In fact, if you have a semi-tropical greenhouse, this crop will feel right at home. Eggplant seeds will not germinate at soil temperatures lower than 75°F, and growth is almost stopped below 60°F. However, eggplants are easier to raise than cucumbers where temperatures are right, because they are not as prone to the molds and mildews that seem to

80

love cukes. Remove the fruits shortly before they reach mature size to keep the plant producing. This crop also likes regular fertilizing. Midgets are available that are great for container gardening. Eggplants, too, should migrate to the house as weather cools.

Peppers come in many varieties to suit many tastes. They are all sensitive to the cold, and to low light levels. Peppers will germinate in fourteen days at a 70°F soil temperature, and plants must be kept in a warm environment—above 65°F—for fruit to set. When the first blossoms appear, place them on the regular feeding schedule. This is one plant that I bring from the garden directly into our house as soon as the nights start to cool down in early September.

Seasoning for the Solstice

J U N E

The climate:
warm to hot,
and there can be less light
in the solar greenhouse
than it had in winter

The chores:
taking care of whatever you've got,
watering,
feeding,
keeping cool,
and multiplying

June is a good month to think about propagating house plants and other perennials. Started now, they will be well-established before the cooler months come again. June is also a good time to plant herbs. Most will grow quite well in containers and in miniature hanging herb gardens in the warm weather greenhouse.

Although most of your thoughts will be turned toward the out-of-doors, don't forget that some seedlings for the cool-weather greenhouse garden (described in July) must be planted before the summer solstice, on June 21.

Some people feel that there is a deep, dark secret to multiplying plants, privy only to those who practice this art. Propagation by layering, grafting, rooting, or cutting are simply other means by which new generations of plants are started. We have already discussed the most common form of propagation used to raise vegetable crops—sowing seeds. There are sometimes reasons, however, for not using seeds to carry on a plant line. Plants often will grow faster when started by an artificial means. In many cases, nature has set conditions that require seeds to go through dormant periods, alternating cold and cool cycles, or a series of other conditions before the seeds will germinate. This can mean a long delay between generations and slow production of stock, and there is no guarantee that off-spring produced sexually—through seeds—will carry all the good traits of the parent stock. Traits evident in parents can get "lost" in the pool of genetic material and not reappear for several generations. (Many of these problems can be overcome for vegetables—see planting techniques, pages 103 to 112).

Fruits, some vegetables such as horseradish, some of the culinary herbs, and many varieties of houseplants are reproduced by *asexual propagation.* After you have propagated your first plants by these methods, you will realize that the only deep dark secret is to have the right controlled environment for your cuttings—and to leave them alone until they are established.

Propagation soils. Plants can be propagated successfully in a variety of soil mixtures. The most popular is the 1–1–1 mix of pasteurized garden loam, peat moss, and inert material (sand, perlite, or vermiculite). The environment of the propagation bed is humid and warm, however, so damping-off can be a major threat to the new plants. The use of a *soilless* medium avoids the problem. These are available commercially or you can make your own by combining equal parts of sphagnum moss with sand or perlite or vermiculite— or you can simply use pure sand, or perlite, or vermiculite. I prefer vermiculite. It is not heavy, and seems to produce better roots for me. Sand should always be coarse to allow air circulation around the newly forming root system.

Equipment. You can spend a fair amount of money here—or make your own. Because the needs are simple, I suggest home industry. Then, if disease hits your plants, you can discard the materials without any feelings of guilt.

A knife is essential, a penknife, a kitchen knife, or any other small knife honed to a fine sharpness. A pocket lighter should be handy to flame-sterilize the knife as you move from one plant to the next. This hinders the spread of disease.

Sieves are also necessary because rooting medium— whether it is soil or some other mix—should have no large particles. If you are using a soil mix or a mix with peat moss, make one sieve using 3/8-inch hardware cloth and another

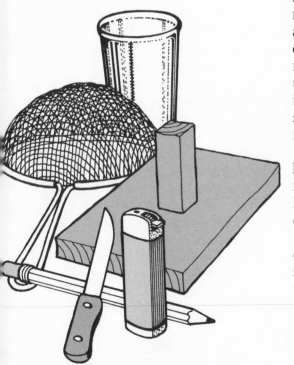

with 1/4-inch wire fly screening. The sieves, whether square or round, should be 12 inches in diameter and about 4 inches deep.

You will also need a variety of tampers to firm the medium around the cuttings and to firm the medium in the boxes or pots. A drinking glass makes a nice pot tamper because it can cover all areas evenly. For flats, make a tamper from a piece of 1 × 4-inch board about 6 inches long. In the middle, nail a small block of wood for a handle. One of the best tampers for firming the soil around a cutting is a pencil with a large eraser. The eraser will not harm the leaf or stem tissue and yet will pack down the medium nicely.

Rooting hormone will cause faster development of the new roots and thus cut down on the likelihood of disease. For rooting softwood or herbaceous cuttings, purchase a can of No. 1 rooting hormone. No. 2 is used for semi-hard woods and No. 3 for hardwoods.

To control the environment around your propagation bed or pot, you will need a propagation case. Here you can really use your ingenuity or spend a lot of money. There is no guarantee that, having spent the money, you will have better results than if you had stuck to simpler things, so try simple things first. Propagating plants need plenty of humidity and a temperature ranging from 60°F to 80°F. If your flats are small, or if you have placed your cuttings in pots, you can make rough frames by cutting and bending coat hangers according to the illustration. Then slip the pots or flats into plastic bags and seal tightly. Air can enter and leave through the polyethylene but moisture cannot. Place the packages where they will receive good, indirect light and the proper temperature. I set mine on top of my water storage barrels in the back of the greenhouse and under a shelf that can provide shade, check them daily for health, and otherwise leave them alone. Unless a problem is observed, the bag should be left sealed for at least three weeks. At that time, you can check for new root formation.

You can also build a controlled-environment box that will serve the purpose nicely. A few dimensions are impor-

PROPAGATION FLAT

tant; otherwise you can suit the shape to your materials. First, the depth of the box should be about 10 inches to allow sufficient headroom above the plants so that the top cover will not touch the cuttings. Second, the box may contain a 2-inch-deep metal tray in which gravel or sand is laid down. When thoroughly wet, this acts as a bottom waterer for the pots and flats. Under the metal tray, and above the Styrofoam-insulated bottom of the box, lay *thermostatically controlled* heating cables. These are available through garden and farm supply stores. The cover can be almost any translucent material: a flat sheet of glass or rigid plastic; polyethylene or vinyl over wire hoops. Its most important function is to prevent the escape of moisture from the box. Although the size of the box should reflect your needs, you might construct a small box first to try your hand at this technique. It will see much use, even if you later go on to a bigger box. One friend uses a large one to start seedlings for her large spring and fall greenhouse gardens, and to start a large number of cuttings for Christmas plant gifts. Otherwise, she uses a small box to start new plants, especially new varieties.

PROPAGATION TECHNIQUES

Cuttings: To make a *stem* cutting, take a small portion—about 3 inches—of a vigorous, healthy stem from the tip of the branch. Remove all but the two to four leaves nearest the tip, plus any flowers or buds. Cut the stem at an angle of 45° with a sharp knife. Dust with rooting hormone and insert 1 to 1¼ inches into 1–1–1 soil mix. Gently tamp down around the stem. Water, cover, and place in a bright (not sunny) warm spot. Check the soil periodically for moisture. Rooting may take three to six weeks.

Leaf cuttings are made with the leaf, including its stem and the swollen leaf bud at the base of the stem. Dust the leaf bud and part of the leaf stem with rooting hormone and insert in moist 1–1–1 soil mix. Cover and place in a bright, warm spot. Check as you do stem cuttings.

Root cuttings are taken when a plant is repotted. Cut some

of the roots (not the root hairs or rootlets) into 2-to-6 inch lengths and place in a flat on moist 1–1–1 soil mix, spaced about 2 inches apart. Cover with sand, then water them. Cover the flat with glass or plastic and place it in a shady spot under a bench. Root cuttings take at least eight weeks to send out new roots, so check the soil periodically for moisture.

Division: This is best done in the greenhouse in the early spring before the plant has a chance to start leafing out. First, prepare a pot or pots as follows: place a layer of coarse material—broken pots or 3/4 inch size stones will do—in such a way that the holes are not plugged. Sift a layer of coarse sand over this. These should fill the pot to no more than a quarter of its height. Fill the pot a third to a half full with moist 1–1–1 soil mix, and tamp. Dig up the plant to be divided. Select parts that contain a growing crown or point, roots, and leaves. These should be vigorous and healthy. Trim out any dead or decayed material. Separate the selected parts. You may have to take a sharp knife to the plant. Cut cleanly; don't hack at it. Insert the plant in the pot, spreading the roots over the soil. Fill the pot with soil mix and tamp. The pot should have about 1-inch clearance between the top of the pot and the top of the soil. Water, and find a warm, bright place to keep it. Check it periodically and keep the soil moist at all times. After a few days, the plant should be able to take its normal amount of sunlight.

87

TIPS FOR ASEXUAL PROPAGATION

The rules for creating new plants by leaf or stem cutting, root cuttings, layering, grafting, division, bulbs, runners and so forth, are not complicated.

1. To fill flats or pots with moist rooting media, fill pot to overflowing, scrape off excess, and use a tamper to firm down the mix evenly. This is not necessary for perlite or vermiculite.

2. Don't try to start new roots in water. Yes, it will work most times. Unfortunately, when you remove the roots from water, they clump together and trying to separate them results in root damage.

3. Do not use root cuttings to raise new grafted plants because the root stock is a different plant from the branches. Root stock for grafted plants is selected for qualities that have little to do with the fruit produced on the plant.

4. If your cuttings do not seem to fare well, it may be that the stock you selected was old. Try taking a *lateral* stem or leaf cutting from near the top of a mature plant. Lateral stems and leaf cuttings root more easily than those taken from the terminal stems and leaves.

5. Removing all except the youngest leaves on the cutting reduces transpiration and still allows the plant to produce food. Flowers, seed pods and other unnecessary materials should also be removed.

6. Stems with large, pithy centers will not root as well as thinner, solid stems.

7. When using rooting hormone, shake some of the powder into a separate dish. Dip the part to be rooted in water, shake to get rid of excess water, and then dip into the rooting hormone (*not* into the can). Shake off excess powder and immediately insert the cutting into the rooting medium.

8. If you are rooting flats, water each row as soon as you have finished it.

9. If you are rooting in a soil medium, use a pencil to make holes for insertion. Place a small amount of sand in each hole to ensure proper drainage. This should not be necessary in soilless media.

THE INDOOR HERB GARDEN

Herbs have a documented history over at least 50,000 years. The earliest evidence comes from the Shanidar cave of Iran where Ralph Solecki, an archaeologist, discovered a burial in which flowers and herbs were interred with the body. Until the advent of modern medicine, it was part of the housewife's job to have a nodding acquaintance with herbs used in cooking and for medicine. Even today, in many of the back villages of Europe and the rest of the world, there is usually some woman (or man) trained in herbal lore by a predecessor, who still cares for those in the village.

The directions for planting, caring for, and harvesting herbs often reflect the ancient traditions as to what had been found to result in the best quality of herb. The inventory of herbs used for various purposes today is very small compared to inventories of the past. Many of the essences and oils once derived from herbs are now produced synthetically, as are many of the medicines. Yet the cultivation and collection of herbs is undergoing a renaissance as cooks again discover the difference between an herb gathered fresh from the garden at peak flavor and the dust found in bottles available in the supermarket. Herbal teas, hot and cold, are also coming into their own as refreshing drinks that have no caffeine.

What is an herb? A mysterious plant? No, herbs can be anything from low-lying, rather scruffy-looking "weeds" to beautiful scented geraniums or roses. Most are easy to grow from seed or cutting and require little attention. They adapt well to container cultivation, and can be raised in the greenhouse, garden and house. Because of their "weediness," container cultivation is, in fact, the best way to grow them. *They have a habit of taking over an area rapidly and becoming pests if not confined.*

Environment. Most herbs are heat-tolerant and prefer warm, sunny, locations—although I have had excellent luck in growing many in a cool greenhouse once they have germinated. Some like a little protection from wind also. Those that shun

MINT TAKES OVER

the cold can be kept on sunny window sills in the house. A few herbs prefer shady but well-lit locations, or partial shading from the sun, during the intense sun of mid-day.

A few varieties cannot take cold below 40°F without being damaged. In general, however, most herbs can tolerate a frost. Their *optimum* night temperature is about 60°F with days in the 80's.

Fertilizer: Like other plants, herbs require more food when growing and undergoing harvest than they do when growth has slowed down, but most like a poorer soil and less food than vegetables do. Feed them every other time you feed your food crops, using the same solution of liquid fish emulsion. If your plants become tall and spindly, you are overfeeding them.

Water: When they are raised outside, herbs with few exceptions seem to like dry soil and growing conditions. Inside, keep them a little dry, soaking the plants well when the top 1/2 to 1 inch of soil (depth varies according to the size and vigor of the plant) has become dry. Do not let the plant wilt; be sure to mist the foliage when you water.

Soil: Many herbs can be grown in the greenhouse 1–1–1 potting soil mix. Directions for exceptions are found in Table 5. For herbs not listed, it is better to start with a light soil, one with more inert material in it than the 1–1–1 mix. For every 5-inch pot, stir in a teaspoon of lime, if necessary to maintain the proper pH, when potting the plant. I add the same amount to plants when I repot, in June when growth is reaching peak and plants go outside for the summer, and also at the end of August as part of bringing them inside.

Propagation: Soak seeds that take a long time to germinate overnight before you plant, to hasten the process. Soil temperature for germination should be 60°F. After sprouting, lower the soil temperature to 50°F.

Herbs may be propagated by plant division, or from cuttings taken from root or stem. Some may be ground-layered by pinning woody stems under flower pots for one growing season. Cuttings do well if you cut about 3 inches of good growth. You do not want new wood, but you can use the woody part of the stem growing just below the new wood. Insert the cutting in a moist medium of 2 parts sand to 1 part vermiculite, thoroughly moistened and drained. Follow the directions for stem propagation. The best method of propagation for each herb can be found on page 94. Where the herb is not listed, consider using stem cuttings.

I propagate most of my herbs asexually when I prune or repot in mid-winter and September. After potting the new plant or repotting a plant, place it in a well-lit but shady location for a week and keep the soil moist rather than wet; the plants should not be allowed to wilt.

Ventilation: Herbs require full natural ventilation, day and night, when night temperatures are above 55 °F (they should not be in drafts, however). Ventilation simulates the drier conditions found in the open. Herbs do not like to be crowded because this allows humidity to build up.

Hardening and Moving the Herb Garden: As you do all other crops raised in the greenhouse, plan to locate herbs in a cold frame for a week when you move them outside in the spring, after night temperatures stay above 55 °F.

Don't forget that herbs can spread prolifically and rapidly. You must pinch off flowers before they can grow to seed. Second reason for pinching flower: leaves harvested before flowering are tastier, more prolific, tenderer. Where the seed is the desired crop, harvest the seed before it dries and complete drying in a paper bag. If the plant propagates by runners, be sure you lift all the runners when you repot in the fall. Remember, your garden may not be the only one invaded.

Here in New Hampshire, I start to bring the herb garden into the greenhouse right after Labor Day and have all herbs in by the middle of September. At this time, herbs are divided where necessary. Remember to place your plants in quarantine for about ten days before bringing them into the greenhouse. They may be susceptible to the common greenhouse pests. Nasturtiums are particularly inviting to aphids. Except for a few of the bigger plants, I raise my greenhouse herbs in large, shallow containers, miniature gardens containing a goodly selection of each variety. Extra gardens are made for future gift-giving.

Pests: Aphids, mealy bugs, whiteflies, and spider mites seem to be the main culprits. Control with one of the sprays mentioned in October and interplant. Misting the leaves when you water also will help.

GROWING TIPS FOR HERBS

1. Never place herb plants over a heat source (except when propagating new plants).

2. Don't overwater, but remember that plants in pots and hanging containers can dry out rapidly.

3. Don't overfeed. You want crisp, vigorous growth.

4. Where the flower and seed are not to be harvested, pinch the flowers ruthlessly to promote bushy growth.

5. Keep plants looking neat. Mist foliage when watering and remove all dead leaves and stems.

6. Make sure pots are adequate in size. If a plant becomes pot-bound, divide the plant and repot.

7. Except for *Florence Fennel,* most herbs get along well together and can be interplanted with other herbs and food crops. See the companion planting chart on page 158 for those that make good insect repellers.

8. Allow space between plants for ventilation and turn plants weekly to promote even foliage growth.

9. Herbs prefer an even heat ranging from a minimum of 55°F to highs of 90°F but can, in most cases, tolerate colder temperatures.

10. Remember that herbs will propagate themselves if given a chance. Keep an eye on them and keep them contained. Do not allow seed to mature on the plant.

11. If you purchase plants, look for vigorous, crisp, healthy growth rather than size. Also check for insects. Never buy a plant if the soil is dry and the plant looks a little wilted.

12. All herbs like light, but some cannot tolerate it in strong doses.

There is a lovely feeling about an herb garden—peaceful, full of tradition, and endless time. Some herbs, when rubbed, release essences, rewarding you with delightful aromas pervading the entire house. Herbs are my room deodorizers and air fresheners. Each is a character, having its own appearance and individual smell. Their friendship is rewarding in so many ways. Enjoy raising these plants!

	Cycle *	Propagation	Soil Conditions, Light	Height	Harvest	Growing Tips
CHIVES (Allium schoenprasum)	P	Seeds, Root division	Rich with lots compost, not excessively acid; full sun.	8"	Foliage; snip & freeze	Repot annually; make divisions at this time; & cut foliage back to crown. Allow to freeze to stimulate new growth. Feed regularly.
GARLIC (Allium sativum)	A	Clove	Same as above.	12"	Bulb	Plant clove in spring 8" apart. Harvest in early fall. Plant early fall for spring harvest. Sow 2" depth.
CHAMOMILE (Anthemis nobilis)	P	Seed or Rooting stem	"Poor", sandy, clayey soils; sun.	6"	Flower	Do not feed or water frequently. Watch for wilting. Keep contained or will take over all "poor soil" areas.
CHERVIL (Anthriscus cerefolium)	A or B	Seed	Loam with no compost; shade.	18" to 24"	Leaves	Seed started in January. Cultivate as you would carrots, harvest like parsley.
TARRAGON (Artemisia dracunculus)	P	Root cuttings, division	Sandy loam, well drained; sun with shade.	24"	Young leaves, stem tips; use fresh	Purchase cuttings. Seeds on market are for Russian Tarragon, a very different plant. Plant in spring 12" apart. Renew every 3 to 4 years. Keep on dry side.
DILL (Anethum graveolens)	A	Seed	Good, well-drained 1-1-1 potting mix; sun.	30"	Leaves, flowers, seeds	Sow thinly directly in pots—do not transplant. Thin to 8". Plant in succession.
BORAGE (Borago officinalis)	A	Seed	1-1-1 potting mix; sun.	24" to 36"	Leaves, flowers	Sow thinly in pots. Make succession plantings. Cutting flowers coarsens stems. Attractive to bees. Do not overwater.
CARAWAY (Carum carvi)	B, P	Seed	1-1-1 potting mix; sun.	24"	Root, seed	Sow seeds thinly in pots. Do not transplant, do not overwater—prefers drier soils.
LEMON VERBENA (Lippia citriodora)	P	Stem cuttings; 1-2" deep runners	1-1-1 potting mix; sun.	24" to 48"	Leaves	A woody shrub that cannot tolerate cold, or cool weather. Raise in warm weather greenhouse summers, or outdoors. Bring into house winters. Lovely lemon fragrance.
MINT (Mentha)	P	Root cuttings planted 1-2" deep; runners	1-1-1 potting mix; sun plus shade.	24" to 36"	Leaves just before flowering	Likes moist soil. Feed regularly. Prune back every fall to stimulate new growth for cool season.
POT MARJORAM (Marjorana onites) also called OREGANO	P	Seed or cuttings	1-1-1 potting mix with a little lime; sun.	8" to 12"	Leaves	Feed occasionally. Divide when plant grows too large. Do not overwater. Seed germination takes 2 weeks.
LEMON BALM (Melissa officinalis)	P	Seed root cuttings division	Seed in soilless potting mix then to 1-1-1 mix; sun.	24"	Dried leaves, flowers stems	Take root cuttings in October. Keep rooting medium moist, warm. Transplant when 1" high to 1-1-1 potting mix. Keep soil moist, feed regularly. Keep sheltered. Seed germination irregular.

*A-annual; B-biennial; P-perennial

Table 5

94

	Cycle *	Propagation	Soil Conditions, Light	Height	Harvest	Growing Tips
SWEET BASIL (*Occimum basilicum*)	A	Seed	1-1-1 mix; filtered sun.	18″	Leaves	Keep soil moist, not wet. Pinch out flower buds to encourage bushing. Feed regularly. Vulnerable to cold.
SCENTED GERANIUMS (*Pelargonium var.*)	P	Leaf cutting early fall from mature plant	Soilless rooting then 1-1-1 mix; sun.	12″ & up	Leaves, flowers, whole plant	Over 50 varieties. Significant differences in scent, flavor, use. Keep cuttings shaded first few days. Keep on dry side. Add bone meal to potting mix (1 qt. to 1 bushel). Pinch tops to produce bushy plants.
PARSLEY (*Petroselinum crispum*)	B	Seed; soak prior to sowing	1-1-1 mix; sun with shade.	8″ to 10″	Leaves	Best treated as annual. Heavy nitrogen user so feed every 2 weeks. Sow thinly and thin to 8″. Do not transplant. Best grown in pots. Can take six weeks to germinate at optimum temperatures (60-70°F).
ANISE (*Pimpinella anisum*)	A	Seed	1 loam 1 inert material ½ compost; sun.	18″ to 24″	Seed	Likes warm soil. Keep on dry side. Grow 2 plants per 8″ pot.
ROSEMARY (*Rosemarinus officinales*)	P	Seed; cuttings; ground layering.	Soilless germinating mix then sandy limed soil; sun or good light.	Bushy shrub	Leaf, plant	Grow several plants for success. Likes a cool spot with a little shade. Mulch with sphagnum moss or sawdust. Fertilize. Add a little lime to pot (3-4 times a year). When pruning, do not cut into woody part of stem. Keep on dry side.
SORRELL, FRENCH (*Rumex scutatus*)	P	Seeds, division	1-1-1 and bone meal; sun.	9″ to 12″	Leaves	Hardy. Takes 2 years to grow from seeds. Needs plenty of watering.
SAGE (*Salvia officinalis*)	P	Seeds; spring cuttings	1-1-1 mix; sun.	6″ to 12″	Leaves	Renew every 2-3 years. Feed regularly; include a teaspoon of lime with every other feeding. Mist leaves frequently.
BURNET (*Sanguisorba minor*)	P	Seed, division	1-1-1 mix 1 tsp. lime per pot; sun.	12″	Leaves	Grow in 12″ shallow pot. Add lime to pot 3-4 times a year. Start about 12 plants, gradually thin by transplanting to 3 per pot.
SAVORY (*Satureia*) **SUMMER** (*horticunsis, L.*) **WINTER** (*montana, L.*)	A, P	Seed or division	Not too rich; 1 loam 1 compost 2 inert material; sun.	18″ to 24″	Leaves	*Summer:* Start in spring. Harvest entire plant as it will not recover from being cut. *Winter:* Transplant early spring and prune back to 4″ above ground to stimulate new growth.
THYME (*Thymus vulgaris*)	P	Cuttings, division, seeds, ground layering	1 loam 1 compost 2 inert material 1 tsp. lime per pot; sun.	6″ to 10″	Leaves	Renew every 2-3 years. Add 1 tsp. lime per pot 3-4 times a year. Grows best in sheltered areas. Many varieties available, each with distinctive character.

*A-annual; B-biennial; P-perennial

Tomatoes for Christmas

J U L Y

The climate:
hot and humid everywhere

The chores:
digging—re-do the soil,
starting more seedlings,
and cleaning up

*T*here you are, all relaxed by the pool or under your favorite shade tree, glass in hand giving off the delightful music of ice cubes clinking together. The outdoor garden is planted and doing well. Weeds are no problem. And visions of a large harvest dance before your eyes. Everything's under control and not much needs to be done. Right? *Wrong!*

July is the month you start to think about Christmas—or rather, the greenhouse garden that will be producing then, making the most of winter light.

Winter greenhouse gardens, grown when days are short, are an exciting challenge to plan and to work in. They test the metal of the gardener and call for bits of ingenuity and imagination, but the rewards are great for just a little effort. There is nothing quite like having the juice of a fresh-picked, vine-ripened tomato dribbling down your chin at Christmas.

There are two distinct kinds of winter greenhouse. The cool winter garden grows when greenhouse temperatures range between freezing and 65°F. Sunlight may be bright at times during the short-lived winter day, but is more often diffused. (Check the weather maps on pages 181-186 for hours of sunlight available to you from October through March.) Plants for this garden must be started shortly after the summer solstice on June 21 to mature before mid-October. The critical factor in this garden is light: select varieties that can do well

97

with low light levels and short day lengths. Coolness or frost must be expected—and often can improve the flavor of cool garden crops.

The winter greenhouse, in parts of the country where temperatures may simulate the summer greenhouse (60°F to 90°F) but where days are short, is another challenging environment. Gardeners working in this environment can grow those plants that like warmth but do not need long daylight for growth. Crops must be started on the same schedule as those for the cool greenhouse garden. Tomatoes and peppers do well here, as will cucumbers and eggplants if night temperatures remain above 60°F. Search for heat-tolerant crops: collards, New Zealand spinach, and turnips for greens, melons, and some of the brassicas newly developed for the south. Avoid cold-tolerant varieties of lettuce, radishes and spinach.

If your winter greenhouse is going to give you tomatoes by Christmas, and salad and vegetable crops this fall, you are going to have to get out of that easy chair, put the glass to one side, and start digging. July, with the change of gardens, is also clean-up and maintenance month. Before the new crops can occupy the ground bed, the soil must be reworked and

nutrients added to it (see March). No plant likes a warmed-over, tasteless meal with no nourishment in it at all. Make up one batch of soil to start seedlings in flats because they can sprout while you dig. They will be ready for the bed as soon as it can receive them.

Do read the chapter (November) on planning the garden before you start to plant. Winter is the traditional time to order seeds, and they should have been stored in tightly sealed jars in a dark, cool, dry place so they will be viable for the cool garden. If you missed it last winter, you may be limited by what is available to you now. A carefully planned garden can help—and give you experience for next year.

Experienced outdoor gardeners may wonder why the garden is started in July and not September. Most plants started in March, after all, need only until June to begin to produce. The difference is that between summer and winter, crops do better if they are allowed to reach maturity before the greenhouse environment becomes cool and days grow short. Plant energy must be directed to maturing the crop rather than the plant, when poor light and cool temperatures slow growth in most plants (from the first of November to about the first of March). The degree to which your greenhouse plants are affected depends upon your location and your greenhouse climate.

The use of raised ground beds for your garden should turn a constraint into an advantage for growing late fall, winter, and early spring crops. They absorb heat and release it slowly, protecting plant root systems from the cold and smoothing out daily temperature swings.

Spinach, tomatoes, peppers and other plants can also be brought in from the outdoor garden as mature, ready-to-produce plants. As fall progresses, bring in kale and other greens that do best after being nipped by frost. Oriental vegetables, lettuce, beet tops, chard, and others love low light; ready them for the November to March garden.

TOMATOES FOR CHRISTMAS

Two methods may be used to propagate fall tomatoes: you may root a leaf pruned from a plant growing in your summer garden, or you can start from seed. I prefer the latter, because plants adapted to the summer garden may not prove hardy in the winter greenhouse.

Cherry tomatoes are an excellent choice for the winter greenhouse. They are more tolerant of adverse conditions, and are vigorous producers of sweet fruit. Most cherry tomatoes are disease-resistant and will continue to set fruit as long as the temperature remains above 50°F. Of the cherry tomato varieties, try Sweet 100's, Pixie, and Tiny Tim. There are others, but I can personally vouch for the above. Most seed houses carry them.

Some seed houses, such as Stokes, sell varieties of tomatoes suitable for forcing in the greenhouse. These are the same varieties used by commercial growers, but don't turn your nose up at them as prime examples of plastic foods. Raised under the right conditions these fruits can be as tasty as the best raised in your garden.

A few seed houses, such as Johnny's Select Seeds in Albion, Maine, sell several types of sub-Arctic tomatoes. These are not great on taste but do make nice tomatoey sauces. I

prefer to grow them outside as an early summer crop to start my batches of sauce. I hope that the sub-Arctics will be improved in taste; they are one of a few types of tomato well adapted to the climate of the cool solar greenhouse.

Schedule. In early July, start five cherry tomato plants. These will be ready by mid-November. After the seedlings have grown for three to four weeks, select the most vigorous plants to carry on for the greenhouse. With just two tomato eaters at home, I find two plants to be sufficient. If you want to try one of the sub-Arctic varieties, start the seeds by August 1, again raising one plant per tomato eater. The sub-Arctics will start bearing by Christmas, and will complement the crop of cherry tomatoes that should still be coming into fruit.

Growing: Summer heat can be as hard on plants as winter cold, so I raise these plants in a cool north room or cellar under a fluorescent light for twelve hours a day until they are strong enough to bear the full sunlight, about four weeks after they sprout. Start the seedlings in a soilless medium in a spot where the temperature will range between 60° and 80°F. As soon as the seeds pop through the medium, place the plants under lights fixed 2 inches above the flats. Temperature should be kept to 60°F if possible. When the plants have grown to ½ inch, transplant them to new flats containing dampened soilless mix. Keep the seedlings on the dry side, watering only when the growing medium has dried out a little, but before the plants wilt.

After three weeks, transplant to small peat pots or paper cups (7 oz.). You should now use a soil mix of 2 parts sphagnum moss/2 parts inert material/1 part rotted compost. Do not use fertilizers. Too much nitrogen will produce a lot of beautiful foliage and not much else. Be sure to transplant the seedlings deeper into the soil each time to promote strong root growth, and don't forget to raise the lights as the plants grow.

When the plants have outgrown these small pots, transplant into the standard 1–1–1 growing medium in larger pots. Reduce the soil temperature to 55°F if possible. The plants

CONTAINERIZED CHERRY TOMATOES

should be transplanted at least one more time before being placed in their permanent locations. Feed no more than once every three weeks with dilute liquid fish emulsion. If the leaves become yellowish, feed a little more often.

The plants should be in the greenhouse by Labor Day at the latest. The containers in which your tomatoes are finally located should be large—about the size of a 1-gallon bucket for the cherry tomatoes, and larger for the sub-Arctics—with at least five or six drainage holes around the base of the bucket.

My plants are finally located hanging root down from the center roof rafter in the middle of the greenhouse garden. Here they receive maximum sunlight and are in a warm microclimate. By the end of November, however, this microclimate is not warm enough every day to support continued blossoming, so I shift my plants into the house where they hang about 1 foot back from a large south window. They continue producing right through the winter and into the spring when they return to the greenhouse.

The mature plants should be watered thoroughly when the top ½ inch of soil has become dry. By November you should be feeding the plant once every three weeks with the dilute liquid fish emulsion.

Harvest. Keep harvesting the tomatoes at the peak of ripeness. Overripe tomatoes encourage mold formation and use more of the plant's energy than is necessary. Some cherry tomatoes, the Sweet 100's for example, are very heavy producers. Watch heavily laden stems for signs of cracking. If you think the stem load too heavy, provide support either by staking and tying or by supporting the limb with a wide-mesh cloth.

Pests. Tomatoes are particularly attractive to whitefly. See October for controls.

THE COOL–WINTER GARDEN

Seed Selection: Plants raised for the summer outdoor garden will not always do well in the fall-winter-spring greenhouse because their light and temperature needs may be too high.

Success lies in selecting plant varieties adapted to your greenhouse environment. Check "Saving your own seeds" page 116, "The greenhouse environment" page 1, and "Planning the greenhouse gardens" page 152, for tips on seed selection.

The Outdoor Seedbed: Seedlings for the winter greenhouse can be started under glass using the techniques described on pages 103 to 112, or they may be started in specially prepared seedbeds in the outdoor garden.

If you plant outside, work the soil thoroughly and finely, and lace it liberally with compost. Keep it light, or seedlings may have a hard time pushing through it. Keep the area moist at all times, and once the seedlings have been transplanted to another part of the bed, mulch around them. Transplanting spaces plants properly for their size and seems to stimulate root growth. Gradually reduce the amount of water given the transplants but don't let them wilt.

It is important to shade the seeded areas *lightly*. Too much strong July sunlight can scorch tender leaves. I usually use a few thinly-leaved branches nailed horizontally to stakes about 1½ to 2 feet above the ground. (Such plants as cucumbers and melons demand full sunlight immediately.) Place a few stones along the edges of the seed bed to act as windbreaks, protecting against drying breezes.

Indoor sprouting: If you raise seedlings for the winter garden in the summer greenhouse, there are a few rules to follow. Be sure the seedling area is well-vented. Seedlings are grown close together and in a hot, humid greenhouse are susceptible to damping-off and other mildew and fungus diseases. Place a small fan near the little plants to stir up the air above them— but remember, a gale will dry them out rapidly. Seedlings should be raised in a spot where light is bright but not necessarily strong.

Unless otherwise indicated in the growing tips and Table 6, water the plants daily and feed weekly with a very dilute fertilizer (½ teaspoon liquid fish emulsion to 1 gallon water)

through August. Transplant to give them the room they need at various stages of growth.

Start seedlings too tender to be transplanted in peat pots. These delicate plants will be part of the container garden, so at transplant time move them into vessels large enough to accommodate the mature plants and plant without removing the peat pots.

Hardening: Plants will have to be hardened off to meet the climate of the winter greenhouse. This is best done by continuous venting during the summer until night temperatures start to fall below 55°F. Soil temperature should remain above 55°F during this time to keep the plants growing. In September and October it will fall naturally to 45° or 50°F over a period of several weeks. Such crops as broccoli and cauliflower cannot tolerate temperatures below 50°F in the adolescent phase of growth, but can be cold-hardened later.

Gradually reduce the amount of water given. Allow the top ½ inch of soil to become dry between waterings, but be careful that plants do not wilt. Humidity levels can be boosted by watering the floor mid-morning and afternoon. Mist the leaves in the morning several times a week to rinse off fungus spores, and to keep leaf pores free of dust.

As you decrease watering, you should also feed the plants less frequently. By September, your plants should be receiving a strong liquid fish emulsion (but no more than 1 tablespoon per gallon of water) every two weeks. Reduce this to every three weeks during October and the first half of November. Then, cut to once a month through the end of February.

Sowing Schedule: Table 6 shows approximate dates for starting winter greenhouse crops. The dates are calculated to allow the plant to reach early vigorous maturity before fall. The plants also recover from harvest at a slower rate in winter, so I usually double the number of seedlings needed for the spring-summer outside garden, in order to get the same production. There should be enough plants to allow you to harvest small amounts from each plant each week.

GROWING TIPS FOR WINTER GREENHOUSE PLANTS

These are exceptions to the general rules for soil, propagation, and transplanting found in Table 6.

Beans require both good light and warm temperatures (70°F days and 50°F nights). Try cold-hardening the plants by gradually reducing temperatures and the amounts of water and fertilizer given. Beans may be interplanted with lettuces and radishes.

In growing beets avoid using much lime to sweeten the soil. Try potash instead. Beets require boron, which can be tied up by lime. Detroit Reds are boron-resistant. Lutz Green Leaf and Park's Green Top Bunching varieties are good for beet tops and will tolerate a fair amount of adverse weather. Overwatering in cold weather can cause root rot.

Brassicas such as broccoli, Brussels sprouts, cauliflower, cabbage, kale, and kohlrabi all will do well in the cool greenhouse. Most, however, take up lots of valuable space and can be grown outside until the weather becomes quite cold. Some brassicas store well in root cellars. Kale, the one exception, is a vigorous producer for the amount of space it requires. Cousins of the American brassicas originating in the Orient are discussed under Oriental vegetables.

Carrots are a must to carry us through those days after the last stored one has disappeared, until the outdoor garden starts producing fresh vegetables again. The seeds can be sown directly on the beds and patted down or covered with the lightest dusting of soil. Cover with plastic to retain heat and moisture; remove it when plants appear, and thin them. Carrots cannot stand hot, dry temperatures, so a warm winter greenhouse may be one place for Southwestern gardeners to raise this crop.

Celery is nice to raise if you can keep your greenhouse above 55°F. Celery requires such a long time to germinate that I bring it into the house to avoid tying up my propagation box. It needs a fluctuating temperature (days 80°F to 60°F nights) to germinate; reduce night temperatures to 50°-55°F after

germination. (Your greenhouse may naturally vibrate between these temperatures.) Start the seed at the end of the hot season and sow successively every eight to twelve weeks depending on your needs. Sow the seeds very thinly on the propagation bedding and press in lightly with a tamper. Cover completely with plastic. Celery requires goodly quantities of food and drink, and must be kept weed free to prevent damping off. L.H. Bailey, in *The Forcing Book* (Macmillan, 1897), found that blanching methods satisfactory for outdoor use caused mold and mildew when used indoors. He achieved the best blanching results by wrapping each plant with brown wrapping paper from lower leaf to soil. Some people think unblanched celery tastes better.

Chard is a delight for the cool greenhouse. It will continue to produce right through cold weather as long as you keep harvesting the *outer* leaves. This is such a versatile crop that you might plant four to six plants per adult in your family. My neighbor still harvests chard from her outdoor bed after several 20°F freezes.

We saw corn raised in residential greenhouses in the Hebrides of Scotland where both days and nights are 40° to 50°F in August and there are few really clear days. In the United States corn is not an exotic vegetable and so should probably not take valuable greenhouse space. If you feel the urge to grow this crop and have a warm house, try raising some of the dwarf varieties.

Leeks, a mild-tasting member of the onion family, are cold-tolerant and require less growing room than onions do. Leeks also make good companion plants for a number of greenhouse plants. Grow them in rich, humusy soil. I sow leek seeds directly into a corner of the ground bed and intersperse them here and there throughout the bed. They seem to take their time germinating and, just when I think I've lost them, they start to straggle up. When planting the seeds, scratch the surface of the soil, sprinkle seeds, and pat down. Water lightly.

Mustard is a long-time Southern favorite that makes a good cool climate greenhouse crop. I usually grow six plants to keep two of us in salad and vegetable greens, as they do not readily recover from severe harvesting in the cool weather. Snip off all forming flowers. Any seed lost on the ground will result in lots of new plants. This is a pesky weed in some areas of the world, choking fields of grain. Tender Green variety, a high-quality import from China, is resistant to hot, dry weather and is slow to seed.

Okra is sensitive to cold weather and soils, and should only be grown where greenhouse soils can be kept above 60°F. To hasten germination, sow in peat pots in early August. Keep in peat pots when moving to the ground bed or containers, as okra does not transplant well. Keep watered but do not over-feed or plants will run to foliage. Remove pods as they mature to promote continuous production. Sudden temperature swings, or hot, dry air that interferes with pollination, can cause buds to drop.

Bunching onions seem to have a strain suited to every climate. In warmer areas this vegetable does well in the out-

LEEKS AND *PAK CHOI*

door garden in the winter. Because they are not stored and their growing season is about half that of the onion, this crop can be grown from seeds. Harvest about sixty days after seeding. For cooler areas, several hardy Orientals are available in addition to the usual onion varieties. Onions are normally cold-tolerant.

Oriental vegetable crops seem to be more resistant to weather vagaries than those we normally grow outdoors, and do well in the low light available during the winter. The low temperatures at which they grow help to keep insect infestations and disease at a minimum. Provide partial shade for these plants. Tuck behind or under other plants. Chinese vegetables are widely used in salads as well as in traditional Chinese dishes and stir-fry cooking. Varieties of Chinese cabbage include: *Michihli, Pai Tsai* (white stalk), and *Wong Bok.* Other brassicas include *Bok* or *Pak Choy, Pe Tsai,* and *Dow Guak. Boy Choy* is similar to celery, *Pe Tsai* to the Chinese cabbages found in the supermarket, and *Dow Guak* is also called Chinese kale or broccoli. A number of seedspeople carry these and other Oriental seed varieties worth trying in the cool weather greenhouse.

Peas are another good crop with strains suited to most greenhouse climates. Cold-resistant varieties cannot be grown in hot areas, where blossoms will not set; most seed catalogs list heat-resistant strains for the warmer climate greenhouse. Sow about fifty seeds every ten to fifteen days for continuous crops. Peas produce their own nitrogen after six weeks so do not feed with nitrogen fertilizers after the fifth week. They do require other nutrients, and should be planted in soil liberally enriched with compost plus a little bone meal, blood meal, and some potash. Edible pod or sugar snap varieties will produce more food in less space and with less waste.

Parsnips, a cold-hardy crop, can be started in May in the greenhouse and transplanted to a deeply dug cold-frame bed after your seedlings have vacated it for the summer. In the fall, after the first good freeze, mulch around the cold frame and around the parsnips inside it. The parsnips are then available all winter long.

109

Radishes will grow in any cool winter greenhouse with very little trouble. Start them about the end of August and sow in succession every two weeks until November. Then, double the amount of seed planted and sow on a monthly schedule until March. Radishes are phototropic. If you live in areas where the winter crop does not bulb up, you may grow radishes under a 40-watt fluorescent lamp or under incandescent lamps. Turn lights on for four hours during the middle of the night. This seems to me to be a little drastic, however; the return on investment is poor. Increasing the amount of space between plants also helps bulbing under poor light conditions. Radishes require a rich, loose soil, and do best when day temperatures remain under 75°F on bright days.

Sowing dates for true spinach will vary according to the greenhouse climate. For winter crops, sow in early September in the northern states, October in central states, and November in southern states. Such heat-resistant varieties as Melody Hybrid and Winter Bloomsdale are available for warmer greenhouses. Melody Hybrid is resistant also to some of the common spinach diseases. If cottonseed meal is used as a fertilizer, add lime to provide the proper pH for nutrient release and uptake by the plants.

New Zealand spinach can be started in the late summer directly in the bed. I find it does not transplant too well, so I sow thinly and keep thinning the plants as they reach maturity. Seed may not germinate unless soaked because the seed may rot in the moist soil before growth can start. This is an early fall and spring crop under glass.

Turnip greens are a cool winter greenhouse crop in northern and high altitude regions, and an outdoor winter crop in the south. Sow seedlings in propagation flats or directly in beds in mid-August. Make succession sowings every three weeks until November, when the light is so short that later sowings will take longer to mature. Tokyo Cross Hybrid has the virtues of producing excellent greens, is resistant to turnip diseases and virus, and matures at a very early date. All turnip strains may be harvested for greens, however.

SEED GERMINATION AND TRANSPLANT SCHEDULE

	Germination		Growing Temp (°F)				
	Time (days)	Soil Temp. (°F)	Day (max.)	Night (min.)	Transplant Spacing	Time to maturity (days)	Comments
BEANS, POLE	4-8	60-85	80	55	4"-5" per pole	60-90	Needs maximum sunlight. Grow mid-green-house in winter or against reflective wall. Beware mildews. Start seeds in August.
BEETS	3-14	65-80	60	40	4" x 4"	45-60 for greens	Soil pH 6.8-8.0 as beets need sweet soil. Can become boron-deficient when excessive lime used. Raise for greens. Cold tolerant. Seeds will produce 4-5 plants per seed. Transplant thinning start mid-summer.
BROCCOLI	3-10	65-80	65	55	18" x 18"	90-120	Soil pH 6.0-7.0. Cold tolerant. Susceptible to temperatures below 50°F just after first true leaves have formed if cold persists. Heavy nitrogen user. Full sun.
BRUSSELS SPROUTS	3-10	65-80	65	55	18" x 18"	90-120	See Broccoli; Brassicas, Gen. Start seeds mid-summer. Full sun.
CARROTS	6-21	50-85	45	65	2" x 2"	70-120	Hot weather, dry soil retards growth as does irregular weather, excessive feeding. Start seed mid-August.
CELERY	10-20	50-68	70	55	12" x 12"	180	Keep seed covered and moist while germinating. Germination improved by causing temperatures to fluctuate between day maximums and night minimums. Heavy feeder and drinker. Some strains require blanching. Start seeds in June and mid-December.
CHARD	3-14	65-85	85	40	6" x 6"	60	Best when nights are cool, days sunny. Growth slows with decreasing daylight. Can transplant from garden for ready crop or plant seeds in late summer. Tolerates both heat and cold.
COLLARDS	3-10	65-85	95	35	6" x 6"	90-100	Heat and cold tolerant. Transplant at 6-8 weeks. Add a little extra manure to each hole when transplanting. A brassica; start seeds in July.
KALE	3-10	65-85	65	35	10" x 10"	120-150	Try bringing plants indoors *after* light frost. Feed with liquid fish emulsion (dilute). Attractive to aphids. Brassica. Start seeds in June.
LEEKS	6-14	60-70	65	35	4" x 4·"	150	Plant in June from seed. When transplanting add a little compost to worked soil. Hill as leek grows. Feed regularly. Cold-tolerant.
MUSTARD	3-7	65-85	85	40	6" x 6"	50-70	Both pot herb and vegetable, depending on use. Heat tolerant but will grow in cool climate in rich, humusy soil. Start seeds early August for fall crop.

Table 6

111

SEED GERMINATION AND TRANSPLANT SCHEDULE

	Germination		Growing Temp (°F)		Transplant Spacing	Time to maturity (days)	Comments
	Time (days)	Soil Temp. (°F)	Day (max.)	Night (min.)			
OKRA	4-14	65-85	95	65	18" x 18"	60-80	For the semi-tropical greenhouse. Start seeds in August in peat pots. Do not overfeed. Full sun.
ONIONS, BUNCHING	6-10	65-70	65	35	1" x 1"	60-70	Start seeds in August and plant in succession. Requires good light to develop so restrict to fall and spring gardens or use light. Oriental varieties do not bulb. Both heat and cold-resistant strains available.
ORIENTAL VEGETABLES	5-7	50-60	60	35	Depends on crop grown	60-90	Includes Chinese varieties of cabbage, broccoli, kale, celery. Requires good light but sensitive to sunlight and heat. Heavy nitrogen users. Start seeds mid-August.
PEAS	5-10	65-70	75	40	2" x 2"	55-70	Use soil with more compost. Use legume inoculant before planting. Cold-tolerant. Some heat-tolerant varieties available. May need trellising. Start sowing mid-August.
RADISHES	4-5	65-70	70	40	2" x 2"	22-30	Cold-tolerant. Plant weekly in succession, sowing directly in bed. May not bulb if light is insufficent. Can be interplanted under and around many crops. Moderate drinker. Start sowing mid-August.
RUTABAGA	see turnip greens						May be raised for winter greens
SPINACH, NEW ZEALAND	5-28	50-86	85	50		55-70	Thrives in warmer greenhouse. Sow seed 2" apart and gradually thin. Keep well-watered. Start seeds the beginning of August.
SPINACH, TRUE	7-21	55-60	60	45	4" x 4"	50	Grows poorly in low light levels. Sow in January for early spring crop. Use nitrogen-rich fertilizer. Water generously.
TURNIP GREENS	3-7	65-85	55	35	6" x 6"	30-60	Consider this for a cold-frame winter crop where frosts are not heavy. Frost improves flavor. Start the end of August.

All temperatures are for soil temperature.
Maturity times will be twice as long in the fall as in the spring as a result of low light levels, short days, and cool temperatures.

The Seeds of Future Generations

AUGUST

The climate:
still hot and humid everywhere—
but think of frost if your
first-frost date
is early

The chores:
identifying plants destined for posterity,
collecting and saving seeds,
taking a long tall drink

*L*ate summer is the same in all parts of the country. In some areas a second outdoor crop has been started in the greenhouse to take advantage of late frost dates. These seedlings can be hardened off and planted outside during August.

Caution: Watch temperature and humidity. Greenhouse temperatures should not go above 90°F. When higher temperatures threaten, you have to treat the greenhouse as you would a child with a fever, to bring the temperature down. Humidity must be at least 40 percent, and 60 percent is optimum. Wash down walls, thermal storage, and floors several times each day to reduce temperature and maintain humidity. Try blowing air over wet cloths as an evaporative cooling system.

As plants mature and the harvest season starts, it is time to give some thought to saving seeds for future gardens—especially if you are interested in growing plants specifically adapted to your greenhouse environment.

In August you should also start planning to bring your outside garden indoors. All tools and equipment should be ready, beds reworked to receive the plants, the "quarantine station" should be clear, and the plan for the cool greenhouse garden finalized. The last seeds for the winter garden should be sown in August according to the schedules on page 111.

The calendar for August is busy. Seedlings should be in-

115

spected daily. Watering and feeding schedules must be maintained. The last week should be devoted to final preparations for bringing the outdoor plants into the greenhouse.

SAVING SEEDS

Horticulturists through the centuries have been ever on the watch for new or improved varieties. As a result we now have vegetables that our ancestors did not have. Many of our current American apple varieties have come into existence in the last two hundred years. Carrots are a nineteenth-century development. The corn of five hundred years ago—or two hundred or even fifty years ago—was far different from the corn we know today. Yet the ancestry of these vegetables can be traced back and the original stock can, in some cases, still be found growing wild.

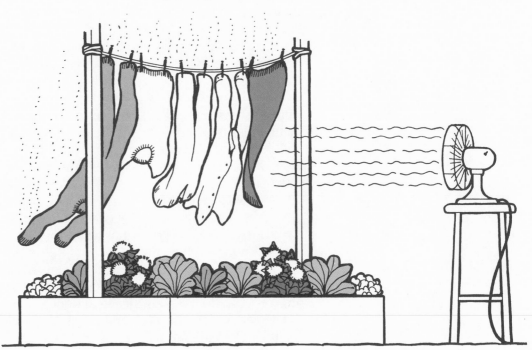

EVAPORATIVE COOLING

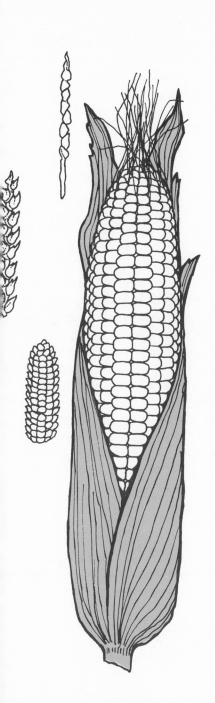

At one time, the gardener and farmer traditionally saved his or her own seeds for next year's garden. Crops could be improved by swapping seeds with neighbors but you certainly couldn't run down to the supermarket or garden store and pick what you needed off the shelf. Few people save seeds now— but greenhouse gardeners should, for a number of reasons. First, you are working with an environment that, in many ways, is unique. Solar greenhouses are individual entities because much of the behavior of each depends on its design and use. When you do find a variety that likes your greenhouse you will want to hang onto it.

Second, you can increase the yield of crops by selecting seeds from healthy, vigorous plants that bear heavy crops either in large numbers or in big sizes.

Third, you may find strains that can overcome some greenhouse problems. As I search for wintering varieties of plants suited to my greenhouse, I find few that are disease-resistant, so I watch for plants that are disease or pest free when the rest of the plants of that kind have problems, and I save those seeds. Look for varieties that do well in the worst climates of both the warm and cool greenhouse; seek out those plants that seem to do well in low light levels.

Part of knowing your greenhouse is understanding what grows well in your indoor garden at various seasons. Observation is important. So is having some idea of what you are looking for in a crop. So is record-keeping (see October). If you plan to save seeds you should know each plant's history, what strain it is, where you purchased the seed, and a few things about how it has grown. You should note whether it is a standard or hybrid strain, with a few details on its expected performance. For purchased seed, all of this information, except for details of growth, is available either in the seed catalog or on the packet.

Hybrid plant strains present a problem to the seed saver. The plant from a first generation hybrid, called F_1 in the catalogs, will not produce seeds that will grow into plants like itself. If possible, select standard varieties when ordering seeds. The old standards, however, are going the way of many good things and are increasingly hard to buy. If you are seriously in-

BAGGING SEED ON THE PLANT

terested in learning to adapt plants to your greenhouse and want to become involved in saving seeds, I refer you to the True Seed Exchange, Kent Whaley, RR 1, Princeton, Mo. 64673. This organization of gardeners intends to preserve and spread many of the old vegetable varieties before they are lost forever. They also experiment with little-known vegetables.

Cross-pollination can be another problem. If a variety cross-pollinates easily, care must be taken to prevent this. Tying a clear plastic bag over the flower *bud* keeps the flower pure and chaste until you are ready to pollinate it by hand. Once pollinated, remove the bag. If the seeds are small, as with carrots and onions, replacing the bag over the fertilized flower shortly before the seed pod matures and turns brown makes seed harvesting easy. Brassica and squash families cross-pollinate readily within the family. In the greenhouse, this can be controlled because plants are fewer in number than they are in the outdoor garden, and flower buds can be kept covered.

It takes several years to develop a new strain of a crop. The seed you saved will, when planted, produce a certain number of desirable plants and some that are not. Each year, new seed must be selected only from plants showing the desired traits, and each year the number of plants that are what you want will increase. When selecting a plant for seed:

• Consider the plant as a whole, even though you are trying to improve only some traits. You may want to improve fruit, but you must think of the plant on which the fruit grows.

• The plant must be disease-free, healthy, and vigorous. Some plant diseases can be transmitted through the seed.

• With root crops, check the root to make sure it has the features you want.

Most garden vegetables are annuals and will produce seed the same year the crop is planted if some of the fruit is allowed to reach maturity. Biennial crops like onions and brassicas produce seed only during the second year of growth.

When you have selected a plant for seed production, tag it so you will not harvest the crop and lose the seed. Some plants that produce heavily can be picked in part, as long as excellent specimens are left to ripen fully on the vine. In all cases, fruit should be fully mature and slightly overripe before it is harvested for seed. In many cases, the stem of the fruit or seed-bearing part of the plant will turn brown and wither when seed is ripe. Allow cucumbers to remain on the vine until they become quite soft so the pulp will separate from the fruit more easily.

Cut open tomatoes and other pulpy fruits and make sure they have the characteristics desired. Place the seeds with whatever pulp you can't separate from them in wooden, glass, or porcelain bowls, and add water. Allow the "soup" to ferment for twenty-four hours, then stir vigorously. A lot of the pulpy matter and light seed will rise to the top and should be discarded. Wash and stir several times. If pulpy matter remains attached to the seeds, let it ferment for another twenty-four hours and repeat the process. Spread the seeds out on some absorbent material and place in a shady place where there is air circulation. When dry (about three weeks), store the seeds in tightly sealed jars, label the jars with type of crop and date harvested, and keep them in a cool, dry, dark place where the temperature does not go above 50°F, and humidity stays between 40 and 50 percent. *Seeds should never be kept in the greenhouse.*

Seeds not "wrapped" in pulpy material may have to be removed from the seed pod in other ways. When the pod is

THE LIFE OF A SEED

Crop	Years Viable
Onion family, parsley	1
Beans, brussel sprouts, kale, okra, peas, peppers	3
Carrot	4
Cabbage, cauliflower, celery, lettuce, radish, spinach turnip, melon	5
Beets, cucumbers, eggplant, muskmelon, tomato, chicory, endive	5+

*Adapted in part from USDA Home & Garden Bulletin No. 202, **Growing Vegetables in the Home Garden.***

Table 7

119

brittle but not thick, the seed may be rubbed out with the fingers. If the seed coat is tough, you may have to thresh it by beating it with a stick. To separate the seed from the chaff, you can winnow it: drop it on to a sheet from a height of 5 to 6 feet when a light breeze is blowing. The breeze will carry away the unwanted husks and stem parts and the heavier seed will fall to the sheet.

If you are in doubt about the viability of any seeds, you may test them. Place ten seeds on thoroughly dampened (but not soaking wet) paper toweling or newspaper. Cover them with a second sheet of the same material and place them in a warm spot for forty-eight to seventy-two hours. (Seeds that ordinarily are difficult to germinate may take longer.) If the seeds are viable, you will see the sprouts. In the pollination process, the flower ova (potential seed) are not all fertilized by the pollen, and testing can determine the percentage of seeds that will sprout, a figure that is fairly constant for that crop that year. It changes from year to year, but not greatly. The germination percentage tells you how many plants you can expect to sprout from your packet of seeds—if you know how many seeds are in the packet to begin with. You then know how many seeds to sow to get the desired number of plants.

SEED PRESERVATION

Even though I calculate the amount of seed I need for each crop carefully and try not to buy too many seeds, I am stymied by seed companies that package them in large quantities. One packet of lettuce seeds would see me through the whole year, indoors and out, and I like five or six varieties of lettuce in my salads. So each year I used to throw out lots of seeds until I learned how to save them. When I am finished sowing a crop, or readying the seeds I saved for storage, I place the packet of seeds in a glass canning jar, one jar for each crop, and label it with the crop and the date purchased. The jar is placed in a cool, dry, dark spot, Then, when I want to sow again, I know how old my seed is, and am sure it has been kept under good conditions. Some seeds will keep for a long time; others must be purchased new each year for best results. Melon seeds seem to do best when they are a year or two old. Test the stored seeds for germination percentages during the winter months, and plant accordingly. If few seeds sprout, order new seeds. Table 7 gives some idea of the length of time seeds of certain crops are viable.

SEPTEMBER

Ferocious Fauna

The climate:
cooling down,
and the days are growing shorter;
in the north be prepared
for frost

The chores:
bringing the outdoors in,
continuing the care of seedlings,
bugging bugs

*B*y now, days are growing noticeably shorter and nights cooler. The southern states may not feel the difference greatly, but northerners are starting to drag out the winter clothing and an extra blanket on the bed at night feels good. Depending on your location and greenhouse, you may have to stop venting at night to maintain adequate soil temperatures for plant growth.

September sees the outdoor harvest season swing into high gear, with all the chores related to food preserving. Plants for the winter greenhouse gardens are moved inside, and that garden settles into its permanent locations.

August and September are often fair times. You may want to enter some of your prize crops in the agricultural section of the fair. Those ribbons sure look great tacked to the wall above the work table—they sort of spur you on when spirits flag.

There is one more chore for September, and it is important! Bug control. Many bugs like the cooler, humid climate of the winter greenhouse. Get to know them so you can nip their activities in the bud rather than waiting for a full-scale invasion to flower. For this reason, September is the time to apply organic control measures to bugs. We don't want to kill the gardener with the bugs, so exercise caution in all measures you take.

123

PESTS AND DISEASE
IN THE SMALL GREENHOUSE

Every greenhouse has bugs, insects, pests, or whatever else you call those animals that get in the way of raising healthy plants. Many growers kill off their bug populations wholesale—the marketplace is full of handy, kill-em-dead sorts of things. But in all populations, bug, human, and other, the good are mixed in with the bad. If the good insects are allowed to survive and work in your glass house, your job of keeping the bad ones in control will be much easier.

Most of the available material on garden pests and plant diseases has been written for the commercial greenhouse grower, who has special types of problems. Commercial growers generally grow a single crop in a greenhouse with critical environmental limits within which these plants will grow. Bugs that feed on that crop have a banquet on hand rather than a snack or a nibble. When the commercial grower has a bug or a problem, control becomes all-out war: smoke bombs, insecticides, and so forth are liberally used. The bug either dies, or becomes so immune to these things that eventually nothing will keep it under control.

Control. Notice that no mention is made of eradicating bugs. Insects have a habit of becoming immune to the nasty chemicals man has devised for their elimination. Now these chemicals are so strong that they are doing away with man and the bugs are hale and hearty! Your best bet is to make it hard for bugs to enter your greenhouse and unpleasant for them to stay.

In the small residential greenhouse, where you are growing a number of different kinds of plants, it is much easier to wage bug control without going to war. Because you will be growing crops primarily for family use, you can interplant, use companion plants, take advantage of biological controls (good bugs), and become friends with your plants.

First rule of thumb: Avoid weakness. Because the only heat supplied to a solar greenhouse is solar, plants must be protected from the weakening effects of cold, or excessive heat. Weaken-

ed plants are disease-prone. For this reason, grow cold-hardy plants in cool winter greenhouses. Heat storage and the use of night insulation, described in solar greenhouse design manuals, may help lessen the shock of temperature change on your plants—and, when temperatures fall to critical levels, heat can be added to the greenhouse in some other form, either thermo-statically controlled heating cables embedded in the soil of the ground bed, or a door or window opened to the house, to share the heat there.

By the same token, excessive heat can weaken a plant during the summer or in the warm winter areas of the country. Grow heat-hardy plants for summer planting and for warm gardens.

Second rule: Keep the air moving. Solar greenhouses are usually well-vented and have good air circulation because this is necessary to their design. Humidities of 70 percent or above encourage disease and, when combined with excess heat, can seriously weaken plants. Opening vents and turning on fans is a necessary part of greenhouse management.

Third rule: Confuse the fauna—mix up the flora. Interplanting is an effective means of pest control. Bugs, looking for a certain kind of plant, are confused by the mixture of odors and colors present in an interplanted garden. Few of them find their way to their targets. Companion planting, a special method of inter-planting that places mutually beneficial plants adjacent to one another, also decreases the likelihood of bug invasions.

The corn-beans-squash grouping is a classic example of good companion planting. Beans (a legume) fix nitrogen, necessary for the growth of corn and squash, into the soil. Corn stalks act as a support for bean growth and as a route to adequate light. Squash, because of its big leaves and dense growth, shades the soil and increases moisture retention.

Many vegetables and herbs act as repellers of insects and inhibitors of disease. For example, members of the onion family—onions, leeks, chives, and garlic—will contribute to the health of neighboring plants and also control pest infestations.

125

Onion also will enhance the production of essential oils in herbs and improve the flavor of nearby vegetables. Companion plants are listed in Table 8.

Fourth rule: Pick winners. Disease-resistant varieties should be selected when ordering seeds for the greenhouse garden. When you plan the garden, keep the following thoughts in mind: order from a seed company that raises its seed stock in a climate similar to your growing climate; be concerned with varieties particularly suited to your greenhouse; and, if your greenhouse is solar-heated, select crops that can stand up to its vagaries. Seeds produced for your outdoor garden environment may not always succeed in your greenhouse. Plants raised from unsuitable seeds will be prone to disease and insect attack.

The well-planned garden will, with proper care, be more disease-resistant. When you have decided what plants you would like to grow, make an accurate plan of your garden (see November for planning help). Use interplanting and companion planting techniques to enhance the best qualities of your stock; then, when ordering seeds and seedlings, order disease-resistant varieties wherever possible.

TIPS FOR PEST AND DISEASE PREVENTION

1. Keep your greenhouse clean. Many pests like trash and weedy areas to hide in when they are not busy eating plants. A vacuum cleaning of cabinets, undersides of benches, and dark corners, as well as the habit of carrying out all trash, are two ways to accomplish this. When storing flats, stack them tipped on end in rows as this lessens the ideal hiding area. Pots should always be stacked after cleaning.

2. Discard all organic material away from the greenhouse. When you weed, pick off dead leaves, thin out seedlings, and so forth, and put them in a container you carry with you (preferably one that can be scoured out and disinfected). Make sure all *undiseased* organic matter goes into the container and from there into your compost pile.

3. If a plant—or plants—become diseased, discard the entire plant. GET RID OF IT! Sick plants should be *burned* because compost pile temperatures are not high enough to kill all disease-causing factors. Some viruses are spread in smoke, however, so if you suspect one of these dunk the whole plant, pot and all, in a very strong Clorox solution. Then wrap it in a water-tight plastic bag and bury it in a *deep* hole.

After handling diseased plants, wash hands, tools, containers, and anything else that may have come in contact with the plant. Ideally, soak these items for several hours in a solution of 1 part chlorine bleach to 10 parts water.

4. Use treated containers and pasteurized or composted soil mixes in your greenhouse. To treat containers, scrub them in soapy water and then leave them to dry in the sun. This will not

sterilize them, but it does seem to inhibit the retention of any disease organisms in the wood. Any wooden flats that have contained diseased plants should be burned.

5. Quarantine any new plants for at least ten days before bringing them into your greenhouse. Check the plant frequently for signs of insects or disease. Be hard-hearted. Don't accept sick plants from friends to be "cured" in your greenhouse. You stand a chance of losing all your plants.

6. Always wash your hands before entering your greenhouse. Wear washable clothes in the greenhouse. Don't enter the greenhouse with mud or dirt on your shoes or clothes. This may seem to be a picky rule, but soil can be a harbinger of all sorts of nasty items that you do not want in your greenhouse. If you do your greenhouse chores in the morning before other work, the best time of the day for the plants, you probably will bring fewer contaminants into the greenhouse.

7. Do not smoke in the greenhouse. Such diseases as Tobacco Mosaic Virus are transported on smoke. Smokers should be especially careful about cleaning up before entering the greenhouse.

8. Keep the hose nozzle off the floor and away from the soil when watering. Do not touch plants with the hose nozzle or hose. If it can be arranged, elevate the hose and use a hanger to secure the nozzle.

9. Take a good look at each plant as you water. Become familiar with each so you will be more aware of any changes occurring. The time to stop an insect or disease is while you can control it by handpicking or by the removal of one plant.

10. Keep a 10-power magnifying glass in the greenhouse. When you find an insect, identify it properly, then take immediate precautions to prevent its spread. Once the pest has become an infestation, you have a more difficult problem on your hands.

BUG SPRAY RECIPES

Many insects attack—or live on—plants, but only certain species seem to be particularly prevalent in the greenhouse. All can be controlled by greenhouse hygiene, healthy plant stock, and various biological/organic methods. Chemical methods of control are not included in this book because they are expensive, contaminate the environment of the greenhouse, and have decreasing effectiveness.

These organic anti-bug recipes have been culled from a variety of resources: books, pamphlets, people, and personal experimentation. I have used some but not all of them. However, I include them so that you can experiment to see which ones work best for you.

Basic Garlic Spray: An excellent spray for sucking insects, effective against a broad range of common greenhouse pests like aphids, whitefly, and spider mites. I have used it extensively on my outside garden to try to control squash bugs when they proved too much for nasturtiums and marigolds. In a blender, chop 3 oz. of garlic bulbs (3 packages) in 2 teaspoons mineral oil (from a drug store or super market). Let this sit in the blender for twenty-four hours. Using slowest blender speed, slowly add 1 pint water in which ¼ cup of oil-based soap, such as Fels Naptha, has been dissolved. When mixed, strain through fine gauze—a nylon stocking will do—and store in a tightly sealed container. This spray must be diluted 1 part garlic solution to 20 parts water for use. Be sure to use this spray on both sides of the leaves. Note: you may need to hold your nose. "Phew!" writes Loretta Powell "—and I'm Italian!"

Red Pepper-Garlic Spray. Simply add 1 tablespoon red pepper to the concentrated garlic spray. Dilute and use as above. Two fresh hot red peppers can be substituted if you prefer.

Chamomile tea. This can be brewed easily using dry chamomile purchased at a health food store. Make the tea strong: brew ¼ cup of the herb in 1 quart boiling water. Cool. Dilute about 1 to 4 with Soapy Water Spray, which helps to hold the chamomile tea on the leaves. An all-purpose spray for mildews.

Soapy Water Spray. Dissolve ½ cup of soap (*not* detergent; Fels Naptha or Ivory Soap are about the only two left on the market) in 1 gallon of water. This can be poured into the earth around the plant or sprayed on both sides of the leaves. Use this spray cautiously because the soap can burn the leaves. I feel that a good rinse does as well: simply spray the whole plant with water or wipe all the leaves with a moist, soft rag. Then pour the soapy water around the base of the plant to discourage a reappearance. This is an all-purpose spray or plant washing solution.

Tobacco Solution. One oldtimer in our family swore by this for any number of cures, for animals or vegetables. Mix about ½ oz. ground-up tobacco—old cigar or cigarette butts, or chewing tobacco—in about 1 quart water. Allow to stand twenty-four hours before spraying on plants. Excellent against thrips. *Tobacco in any form is dangerous.* This spray, like its commercial cousin Black Leaf 40, is not to be fooled with. It is a last resort. Discard any remaining liquid after the plants have been sprayed. It's easy to make a new batch.

Buttermilk and Wheat Flour Spray. When you cannot obtain ladybugs, and spider mites are eating your crops, try this: Mix ½ cup of buttermilk with 4 cups of wheat flour in 5 gallons of water. Sprinkle on infested leaves. I had to use this once and found it to be satisfactory, but I much prefer ladybugs.

Diatomaceous Earth. The silica skeletons of these single-celled sea-faring animals are an excellent control for chewing insects as well as any other soft-bodied pests. The silica crystals pierce the soft bodies and they dehydrate.

COMMON GREENHOUSE PESTS AND DISEASES

Solar greenhouse growers—or growers in any kind of greenhouse for that matter—need a quick working knowledge of the wild life they are most likely to meet in the greenhouse partly because (again) early prevention is better than painful cure, and

ALL INSECTS SHOWN LARGER
THAN LIFE

partly because solar greenhouses are almost always in close proximity to living spaces, attached to houses or actually integrated into them. To avoid sharing living quarters with swarms of uninvited and unwelcome guests, this rule of thumb applies: know the enemy, and get rid of him early.

Descriptions of pests can be difficult. Aphids, for instance are a large class of very small sucking insects that have a number of traits in common. Color can vary widely, as can size, habit, and favorite food. Fortunately, under a hand magnifying lens, it is generally possible to tell them apart. When unsure of the identity of any bugs living in your garden, try the bug specialist or entymologist at the biology or horticultural department of the nearest college or university, or the county or state agricultural extension service.

APHID AND NYMPH

Aphid, a sucking insect that secretes a "honey-dew" attractive to ants: Aphids come in several colors: greenish-yellow, shiny dark brown, pinkish-green, or yellow with a purple spot. Leaves under attack by aphids will curl or pucker around the edges and along leaf ribs, and young leaves will grow deformed. Root aphids are detected by a white wooly mass on the root system of the plant or in the surrounding soil. Root aphids cause root wilt, and are detected when the plant starts to droop. The aphid's life cycle lasts twenty to thirty days, so whatever measures are taken to contain and control an infestation must be carried out over at least one life cycle and preferably longer. For small infestations, gently rub the leaf between thumb and forefinger to squash the bugs. In large infestations, it is possible for the pest to "disappear" from the greenhouse at the end of the life-cycle only to reappear a few days later in even greater numbers. Aphids can be controlled with ladybugs, spiders, strips of aluminum foil laid between plants, and by sage, rosemary, chives, garlic, and onions planted as companions. The garlic/oil spray is helpful.

Garden centipedes feed on the roots of plants. They prefer soil rich in organic matter. These pests are soft, white, about 1/2 inch long, travel in large numbers and can move very fast.

131

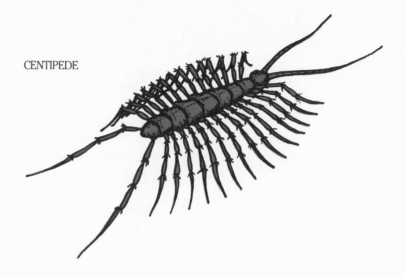

CENTIPEDE

Adults have twelve pairs of legs when fully grown. Check the root system of any plant that is wilting or droopy. To control, mix tobacco juice spray in soapy water and drench around the top of the pot holding the plant.

Gnats, fungus gnats, or root gnats. These small blackish flies feed on organic matter, plant roots, and succulent stems. The larva stage is the most dangerous to plants. Larvae are about 1/4 inch long, yellowish–white with black heads. Plants can be sprayed with a tobacco juice-water solution.

Leaf miners: These insect larvae invade leaves. Beware of yellowing foliage, especially if tunnels can be seen through the surface of the leaf. The larva are yellow and very small. Best control is to hand–pick all infected foliage and burn it.

Leaf rollers and leaf tiers: The Strawberry Leaf Roller is a particular pest of strawberries. Note any folded and webbed leaves. The larva is a 1/2-inch-long yellow-green or brown-green caterpillar. The adult is a red or brown moth with approximately 1/2-inch wingspan. Leaf rollers are best prevented by screening all openings. If an infestation occurs, handpick all

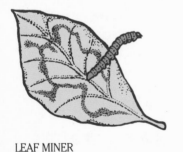

LEAF MINER

LEAF ROLLER

MEALY BUG

SOWBUG

SPIDER MITE

infected leaves and burn. Rotenone, available at most garden and farm supply stores, will kill any eggs when dusted on the underpart of the plant leaves.

Mealy bugs, soft bodied, 1/5-to-1/3-inch-long slow-moving insects that, like the aphid, secrete a sweet chemical to attract ants: This honey-dew also attracts a black fungus growth. White filaments covering the body make the mealy bug look like a miniature tuft of cotton on the undersides of leaves. They are sap suckers, so watch for droopy, wilting plants and leaves. An underground variety will attack plant roots. To control, use a laundry soap or tobacco juice spray on the undersides of infested leaves. For a small invasion, touch the bug with a cotton swab dipped in rubbing alcohol.

Millipedes, worm-like insects up to 1 inch long with two pairs of legs per body segment: Millipedes like organic matter in humid areas and often will attack plant roots and sprouting seeds. When disturbed, they coil up. To control, use a tobacco-laundry soap spray.

Sowbugs or Pillbugs, crustaceans (same family as the much-desired lobster!) that prefer dark places, and damp humus-type soils: They feed primarily on decaying vegetation, rotting wood, and manure but also will gnaw into the stems and crowns of many plants. When disturbed, a sowbug runs for cover while the pillbug curls up. To control, do not leave decaying matter in the greenhouse. Invert a hollowed-out half of a potato near the infested area. Crush those trapped inside and replace with a new potato half.

Spider mites, often detected as tiny grains similar to red pepper on the undersides of leaves, but also may be tan or greenish-white: The two-spotted mite is a perennial greenhouse pest, especially in hot weather. Be aware of stippled leaves, plant distortion, dead tissue, webbing at leaf tips, and a general droopiness. It is necessary to use a magnifying glass to see spider mites, or if you suspect an invasion, hold a piece of

133

white paper under a leaf and tap it. If you can see the tiny grain-sized insects, then you have a spider mite problem. Temperature and humidity control are important. Mites prefer a warm, dry environment, so move your greenhouse climate to the cool, damp side. The cool, damp environment also favors such mite predators as the ladybug or predatory mite, both of which can be purchased commercially. For serious infestations, use ladybugs. If ladybugs are not available, the Abraham's *Organic Gardening Under Glass* recommends a wheat flour-buttermilk spray.

Nematodes (eel worms): Microscopic round worms, they occur in all soils. They attack the roots, leaves, and buds of plants, making them vulnerable to other plant diseases. Nematodes feed within the leaf or bud, producing a water-logged foliage. An infestation results in stunted, crinkled leaves and small flowers, and may also cause galls (lumps) on roots. Pumpkin seedlings are good indicators as infected plants will form galls after three to four weeks. To prevent, never plant obviously infected or unhealthy seedlings. Resistant varieties are available. The worm will spread with water, so spray soil only, taking care that leaves are not wet. Nematodes especially like tomatoes, all beans, squash, peppers, okra, melons, lettuce, carrots, and cucumbers. They do not like radishes, mustard, turnips, onions, or corn. Dwarf marigolds have a limited success in controlling them.

Plant bugs: The Tarnished Plant Bug is the greenhouse pest. Other varieties do their dirty work outside. In the nymph (young) stage it may be mistaken for a small aphid. Adults are small, flat, oval, and a shiny metallic brown or green with black spots located on the throat and abdomen. Tarnished Plant Bugs inject a poison into the plant while feeding on it. Particular favorites include beans, beets, and cucumber. If you also grow cabbage in your greenhouse, this joins the list. Wait until the bugs become active during the day, then dust with Sabadilla powder. This may or may not help. If it does not, try garlic-red pepper spray.

SCALE INSECTS

Scale insects: If you grow any large-leafed plants in your greenhouse, scale could be a problem. These bugs are often legless, may be armored or soft-bodied, circular, oval, or oystershell-like in shape, and 1/8 inch to 1/2 inch in diameter. In addition to sucking the juices from leaf and stem, they inject a poison into the plants that causes them to wither. Scales secrete a honey-dew that attracts ants and sooty mold, adding insult to injury as far as the plant is concerned. A small infestation may be controlled by hand-picking infected parts and burning them. Where they occur in large numbers, take a rag and squash them right on the leaf or stem.

Slugs and snails: Can be a major problem in the greenhouse where the climate is right—humid—and there may be dark corners, the underside of flats, and many other choice hiding places. The best prevention is cleanliness. Keep the greenhouse clean, ventilated, and free of hiding places where possible. Don't bring in pots, flats, or other things that have been sitting on or near the ground, until they have been scrubbed well and disinfected with chlorine bleach solution. Then put in the sun, off the ground for a few days. When storing pots, turn them upside down and stack in a place where air circulation can prevent humidity build-up. Flats should be stored resting on edge in dry places.

Slugs and snails can lay eggs all year, and will increase in population dramatically if not controlled. Eggs are colorless, watery, and gelatinous, about 1/8 inch to 1/4 inch long. A cool greenhouse temperature slows them down somewhat and delays hatching of the eggs. This is one big advantage of the solar greenhouse, where night temperatures are usually on the cool side. If snails persist, do some night detecting with a flashlight. When you find one, sprinkle a little table salt on it. Or put some rubbing alcohol or beer in a very shallow container under a bench. The yeasty smell of beer attracts them; they climb in and drown. Baker's yeast, dissolved with a little sugar in water to a fairly dilute solution will do the same thing. This should be renewed when the yeasty odor is no longer noticeable.

SLUG AND SNAIL

135

Thrips are another microscopic pest that have found their way into most gardens. Use a hand lens to look for their two pairs of fringed wings and short antennae. Thrips are suckers; watch for leaves turning silvery and then withering. Fruits will bear scars. This bug seems to have a universal appetite, and will dine happily on vegetables, if flowers or fruit are not available. Several controls can be used. Place strips of aluminum foil near low plants, or use garlic and red pepper, or tobacco juice sprays. Rotenone will control an infestation but, because it is a dust, it is difficult to control in a small area. Use it only if you seem to have a greenhouse-wide invasion.

Weevils are beetles whose heads are prolonged into snouts. They are night feeders, so you may not see them during the day—only the evidence that they have been around. Of the many weevil varieties, several are of concern to the greenhouse grower. Carrot weevils are copper colored, 1/8 inch long, and are whitish grubs in the larva stage. They harbor in garden debris, so cleanliness is the first step in prevention. They prefer celery, carrots, parsnips, and parsley. In general, they may be found east of Colorado. Vegetable weevils are buff-colored in the adult stage, and have a V on the wing covers. The larva range in color from cream to green with yellow heads. These insects start at the crown of a plant and work their way down, leaving only the stem and leaf mid-rib. Members of the brassica family, beets, lettuce, onions, and tomatoes, are preferred foods. Their habitat is widely distributed.

The best outdoor control is to rotate crops, but this is not possible in the greenhouse. Deep-digging ground beds and soil-filled planting benches twice a year when you are adjusting your soils is one way to destroy the larvae. Screened greenhouse openings help to prevent new ones from entering. If you do find weevils, or signs of them, hand-pick and destroy, and spray the plants with a hot pepper solution.

Whiteflies are the bane of every greenhouse grower. If you see one, you've probably got several hundred on your plants. If

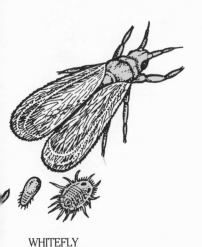

WHITEFLY

you can spot more, you may have a major infestation. The best way to find out how extensive the problem is, is to touch the leaves of plants and watch for clouds of very small flies. All stages can be found on the undersides of leaves: spindle-shaped eggs, yellow crawlers, and white-winged adults. Watch for discolored leaves or sooty mold that develops on a secreted honey-dew.

The whitefly reproductive cycle lasts for thirty days, so any attempt at control must go on for at least that long. To help lower the population, hold the nozzle of your vacuum cleaner next to an infested plant, shake it, and vacuum up any that fly off. This must be done daily. *Encarsia formosa,* a tiny wasp, feeds on whitefly with an insatiable appetite. It likes the temperature to be above 65°F, so unless you can, in some way, maintain this temperature, you cannot use this control. The synthetic pyrethrum "Green" will control all stages of whitefly but must be used cautiously: do not use when the temperature is above 80°F or when plants are dry because it will burn and spot leaves.

A more permanent control is to make some "daisies" by painting 1 foot square by 1 inch thick blocks of wood with Rustoleum 659 yellow paint. Coat the colored boards with a trapping agent such as Tanglefoot, Ced-O-Flora, or Tacktrap. When you shake an infested plant, the flies will swarm to the "daisy" and be trapped. When the board is full, wipe off and recoat. The boards should be hung in the midst of the plants, about midway between top and bottom. They can be placed on sticks or enclosed in greenwire cages that have 2 inch square mesh openings, four treated boards for every 150 square feet of greenhouse floor.

Ladybugs also will control whitefly, and several of the sprays are useful. Be sure to spray both sides of the leaves.

FUNGI

In addition to common pests, there are several diseases and fungi of which you should be aware.

Damping off is a fungus that affects seedlings dramatically. Healthy plants just keel over and die. This can be prevented by using pasteurized soil mixes when starting seedlings. To control, reduce the amount of water used and make sure ventilation is adequate to prevent a build-up in humidity. Peat moss contains a natural inhibitor so, if you prepare your own soil mix, be sure to include some. Some soilless potting mixes already contain peat moss.

Downy mildew or **Powdery mildew** can quickly take over plants. Downy mildew is a white fungus found on the underside of the leaf while the powdery mildew is a white or greyish fungus found on leaf tips. As soon as either is spotted, remove all infected vegetation. Baking soda sprinkled on the leaves may control it, but a fungus can spread so rapidly to other plants that harsh as it may sound, you are far better off getting rid of the infected plants immediately than fooling around with remedies. Tea made of either chives or chamomile may prevent mildew.

Grey mold covers all parts of the plant with a hairy, furry gray covering.

DISEASES

The various stem and root-rotting diseases can be best prevented by watching humidity levels, watering habits, and proper planting techniques. By this, I mean that plants must be given breathing space, proper diets, and careful tending. Mildews, molds, and rotting plants are all signs that ventilation is inadequate and that plants are not able to stand up to the molds and fungi that are found everywhere.

Cucumber or Tobacco Mosaic Virus, infectious to cucumbers, or to tomatoes and peppers: yellow mottled leaves, stunted growth, and distorted leaf growth. Tobacco Mosaic is readily transmitted from tobacco or tobacco products by smoke or nicotine-stained fingers. Best prevention is to avoid smoking in the greenhouse and to wash hands thoroughly before handling plants if you are a smoker. If either virus does appear in your greenhouse, destroy all plants and dispose of the corpses very carefully (do *not* burn; bury deep!).

Fusarium and Verticullum wilts, fungal diseases that result in wilting of the plant after leaves turn yellow: Many plant species are now wilt-resistant. The best prevention is to select these special varieties.

OCTOBER

The climate:
days will be short,
nights cooling—
and the earth is getting
chilly

The chores:
preparing for winter with
caulk gun and
weatherstripping;
the end of the garden comes in;
keeping records,
summarizing the year;
and growing mellow

*B*y the middle of October, days will be too short to mature crops. Such crops as radishes, with short maturation times, can be sown until October 1, but after that poor light prevents formation of the bulb. Night temperatures definitely will have cooled down, lessening the need for night ventilation in all but those climates that have warm daytime temperatures.

With the winter gardens in place and perking along nicely and harvests of outdoor-grown produce slowing down, it is time to enjoy that drink we missed in July. Let's make it brandy to celebrate the completion of a successful season. As we lean back in a comfortable chair and put our feet up, we can use this time to contemplate. What do we know about our greenhouse? What do we need to know that we don't. How can we find this out? What made our successes? And don't forget the failures—lessons can be learned here, too. Just how did each crop fare, and what factors influenced the yields? Because November is a good time to order seed catalogs, we should take our backward glance now and be ready to plan our garden when the wishbooks arrive. If you find it hard to remember whether it was the cabbages or the broccoli that did so well, or which spot got the best light, it is time to introduce record keeping. Record keeping is part of the reflective process. The serious gardener keeps several types, each with a function and use in planning future gardens.

KEEPING RECORDS

Now, the record-keeping part of gardening may sound a bit dull and may seem more of a bother than it is worth but—after twenty-five years of gardening—I still feel the need to refer to my gardening notes about this time of the year.

Every gardener should keep a *daily log*. Only a small spiral notebook and a stub of pencil are required. Keep the notebook in the basket of tools you use in the garden or hang it by the door to the greenhouse where it will remind you to make notes. However you arrange it, try to enter some observations in the book each day, notes on the weather, temperature outside the greenhouse as well as inside, comments on humidity, cloud cover, and outdoor wind speed. If you are monitoring your greenhouse, some of this information will be recorded on your data sheets and need not be copied here—but when it comes to finding out why the eggplant took so long to blossom, those notes on six consecutive days of cool, overcast skies may help to explain.

Note when you feed and water the plants. I normally water daily during the summer, so I don't record this watering schedule unless it changes. The day you are scheduled to feed your plants might also be the day for the office picnic, and the task is forgotten in the flurry of preparation. Note this, as well as the date when you finally did feed them.

Keep track of the performance of the various crops: how long did it take for them to sprout? How many germinated? When did they first blossom? Bear fruit? How heavy was the harvest? Was your feeding and watering schedule satisfactory or did the plants become susceptible to disease? The daily log records tasks accomplished and helps to remind you when they are due to be repeated.

Finally, include commentary. Philosophize if you are so inclined. If something is not going right, note it down; if a crop is doing better than your wildest expectations, that is also important. Sometimes, when I am trying to decide between two equally good producers, a comment written last year may help me to make the decision.

A PAGE FROM
A GREENHOUSE LOGBOOK

July 1 **Started:**
eggplant 8 seeds
Brussels sprouts 6 seeds
collards 8 seeds
pole beans 6 seeds
celery 16 seeds
Chinese cabbage 10 seeds
peppers 8 seeds
okra 8 seeds
leeks–lots
Started zucchini, cukes, watermelon
in peat pots using peat moss only. 2
seeds per pot; on north bench.

Weather: Overcast but bright all day.
Max 80°F, Min 60°F. Very humid;
breeze from SW. Did not water
plants; still quite wet from yesterday.

July 2 Started organizing to dig up ground
bed. Took down south bench and
moved it out. Moved all plants to cold
frame or north bench. Shaded cold
frames with wooden slatted shades.
Took top 3″ of soil off bed and put
in compost pile. Fed all plants with
liquid fish emulsion (1 tablespoon
per gallon water).

Weather: Clear and cool after early
morning shower. Max 75°F, Min
55°F.

July 3, 4 Brought in new compost, sawdust from barn floor. Redug bed, worked in new compost, manure, peat moss. Final pH 6 so added a sprinkling of wood ash. Watered bed.

Weather: Clear both days. Temp on 3rd: Max 80°F, Min 56°F. 4th: 83°F, Min 62°F.

July 5 Watered bed. Brought plants and flats back inside from cold frame. Placed on ground bed for now. Replaced broken glass, started getting ready to paint later this month. Some scraping.

Weather: Cloudy after 11:30 am. Max 84°F, Min 60°F.

July 6 Made soil mix for tomatoes: 1–1–1. First true leaves out.

Weather: Mostly cloudy; Max 83°F, Min 57°F, Humid.

July 7 Transplant tomatoes. Discard 1 seedling—spindly. Put into 3″ pots and placed in central part of ground bed along south edge. Watered ground bed, including under all flats and plants.

Weather: Cleared by 10 am. Max 82°F, Min 57°F; Humid.

July 8   Plants sown 7/1 coming up. Moved
all flats but leeks to ground bed,
north side. Good light, but not
max sun.

Weather: Clear about 10:30 am. Max
83 °F, Min 68 °F. Outside, got more
humid as day progressed.

In addition to the daily log, I maintain a *history card* on
each variety of plant I grow. I may have half a dozen cards on
tomatoes because I am trying that many varieties. Each contains the name of the crop, the variety, where and when the
seed was purchased, all the planting and transplanting information (dates, medium, growth conditions). Feeding and watering
schedules if they differ from the regular greenhouse schedule,
blossom time, fruit set, and yield, are a part of it. And I always
note the way the plant adapted to my garden. This provides a
detailed life history of each crop. Combined with the commentary in the log, it should encourage conclusions relating to the
success of the crop and why it succeeded—or failed. The experimenter can set the stage for change next year. Within those
limits that are controllable, results can be compared from year
to year.

```
Tomato, Cherry
Tiny Tim


      Johnny's Select Seeds    1980
      6/27:  6 seeds planted in 6-pack; peat moss; propagation bag. North
             bench site. No soil heat.
      7/3:   4 plants have germinated. Moved to center front ground bed;
             good light, no full sun.
      7/7:   transplanted to 3" pots; south central ground bed. No full sun.
      7/21:  transplanted to ground bed; North central location. Set
             deeper; fed.
      8/15:  transplant again in ground bed. Same location. Set deeper; fed.
      8/31:  transplant into 1-gallon hanging pot. Located 4 feet from
             ground on post. On regular feeding schedule.
      9/7:   first blossoms.
      9/28:  Moved to rafter in center of greenhouse. Tomatoes well
             started.
```

HISTORY CARD

There is one last card to fill out. I call it my *handy reference card* because a summary of the information detailed elsewhere is condensed here, handy for ordering. If I did not like a crop, I simply say, "Do not order again; takes too long to mature," or something similar.

```
Tomatoes


1978:
Tiny Tim: Results excellent. Taste very good. Heavy yields inside & out.
Coldset: Good producer. Taste strong. OK canner. Very early yields.
Marglobe: Results excellent. Eating & Canning. Heavy yields.
Roma VF: Excellent paste. Heavy yields from mid-Sept.  } Both keep well
San Marzano: Excellent but yields not as heavy as Roma. }  on the vine.

1979:
Pixie: As good as Tiny Tim.
Tiny Tim: Volunteers transplanted to bed. Excellent as always.
Marglobe: Heavy yields for canning.
New Yorker: Fruits later than Marglobe. Heavy yields for canning, eating.
Roma VF: Heavy yields again.  } Combining these two with Marglobe, New Yorker,
San Marzano: Heavy yields.   } made an excellent sauce. Nice & thick.

1980:
Sweet 100's: Excellent in greenhouse. Producing right through winter.
Tiny Tim: Tried in greenhouse; not as good as Sweet 100's.
Marglobe: Adverse weather delayed fruit set; crop small this year.
New Yorker: Yields better than Marglobe, but not up to last year.
Weather bad for all crops in outdoor garden as well as in greenhouse. Cloud
cover decreased available light; too much rain then not enough. Seedlings for
indoor gardens off to a bad start.
```

HANDY REFERENCE CARD

These bits of information, log books, and cards should be kept from year to year. After a while you will be able to use them much as a professor uses his or her research books and reports, for annual updates of familiar lectures. The data will give you a full-color picture of your garden—in words.

Two other kinds of information should be part of your permanent set of records. The first is the set of graphs, described on pages 23 to 24, that defines the environment of your particular greenhouse and details its microclimates—the results of the monitoring discussed in February. These are updated periodically as you check thermometers and note the levels of light, and kept with your permanent records.

The second is your monthly calendar. It is probably smudged, scribbled-on, and water-spotted by the end of the growing year, but it will be invaluable in helping you to plan next year's garden and to draw up next year's calendar.

So it is described in November (page 159) where next year's plans are made.

BRINGING THE OUTSIDE GARDEN INTO THE GREENHOUSE

The actual moment when you begin to bring bits of the outdoor garden inside for the winter will depend upon your earliest frost date and on how severe that first frost will be. In the north and in high altitudes, mid-September seems to be first-frost time. In the south it may be another couple of months later. Whatever the date, set a time about two weeks before the frost for moving the garden. You will need at least two weeks to pot or repot plants, set them in quarantine (for a week or more if you can), and locate them in their final growing places.

The ground bed and other growing areas should have been renewed by the end of July and are now ready for the winter greenhouse garden. Seedlings started for this garden should be in place before plants are brought in from the outside garden, to give them a good start. Follow the plan you conceived in July so you will know where everything is and can rest assured that you have planted enough.

Bring in the perennial plants you took outside in the spring, tender fruits in their containers, herbs for the kitchen, prize vegetables that still have a lot of life left and can stand the climate if it is cool, and plants that are coming to fruition too late to reach maturity. You will have to be selective. There may be room for a few exceptions, but don't try to bring everything into the greenhouse. It's a temptation to dig up all those beautiful, vigorously producing plants and keep them going in the fall greenhouse. But you would weaken them right at the time each needs all its strength to mature its fruit, and they would be in poor condition to face the rigors of the winter in the greenhouse. (You can keep these plants going a long time in the outdoor garden by protecting them from frost with plastic or cloths at night.)

Most of my fall/winter crops are grown in a ground bed, which makes potting them first seem odd. However, this allows

QUARANTINE *OUTSIDE* THE
GREENHOUSE

me to examine the whole plant carefully over a period of time for general health, and the effort is worth it. It also gives the plants time to make the transition into the greenhouse climate by entering the protection of the screened porch or other enclosed area first.

Some crops require a bit of frost to develop their best taste. Others need low temperatures to complete their annual cycle. Leave these plants outside until they have gone through the period of frost or freeze that meets their requirements. As you handle each plant for potting, check the root system for damage, mildew, or other signs of disease. Trim away dead vegetation, and mist the foliage well to remove all pests. If the plant needs dividing, now is a convenient time to do this. If a plant is infested and the bugs won't stay away, spray it with one of the organic sprays recommended in September. Keep

148

it under observation and if the problem persists, discard the plant.

Those plants that spent the summer in pots and will remain in them should be repotted. Divide the plant if it needs dividing. Fruit trees and vines should receive a top dressing of compost plus whatever else they need in the way of food (see April). The old top dressing should go out to the compost pile. It still has valuable organic materials.

If you consider October as a time to exercise preventive care, doing all those things that will start the plant off right, then your approach will be correct. A sick or weak plant will have problems in the difficult climate of the winter greenhouse.

NOVEMBER

**The Promise
in the Seed**

The climate:
dark. the garden is noticibly slow and soil temperatures are low. Some plants are dormant, although during the day the sun is more intense because it is low in the sky

The chores:
planning; ordering seed catalogs and laying out next year's garden; plotting time; stirring up greenhouse air; and nursing the status quo

*T*he northern hemisphere enters the winter season, though the official first day of winter is still weeks away. Crops produce slower, and take longer to recover from a harvest. Growth is measured in millimeters rather than inches, and may be imperceptible. Depending upon the amount of sun you get in the form of direct, heat-giving solar radiation, your greenhouse soil temperatures may range from the low 50°s into the 70°s, which will affect the well-being of your crops. The differences between the winter garden where greenhouse climates are warm and the cool-climate garden become quite evident. Tomatoes and peppers, for example, will blossom and set where temperatures are above 60°F, but not where it is cooler.

The winter garden still requires a few minutes of your time daily. Check for insects, disease, and poor health in plants. Maintain regular water and feeding schedules, but on a limited basis (see page 105 for care of winter garden plants).

On dim days, seedlings may need artificial light. Because seedlings are interplanted, and the *quality* of light each plant requires may differ, I sometimes use one incandescent lamp and one 40-watt fluorescent lamp to provide the full spectrum. Incandescents, however, also add heat to the microclimate, so take it into account. When adding any light to the greenhouse, use light-reflective shades to get every bit of use from it.

151

Don't leave lights on twenty-four hours a day. Plants require a period of darkness to convert sugars produced during the day into the starches and proteins used for growth. Unless special situations dictate otherwise, limit total daylight plus artificial light to fourteen hours maximum per day.

November is the time to anticipate spring, planning for next year in the greenhouse. The records you've been keeping and last year's calendar will help you to decide what was successful in the greenhouse, and what to grow for next year. This month order seed catalogs. Then, once you know the types of plants that do well, and what environmental conditions you are working in, you can lay out the garden and order seed.

PLANS AND PLOTS

Gardens should be planned on paper. Interplanting and companion planting, two techniques that increase yields and protect plants against disease and bug infestations, can be complex if the garden is not planned in advance. Planning on paper also gives you a permanent record of what was planted, and where it was planted, for each year, and can be of help when you try to figure out why a crop was a startling success or a dismal failure—it may have been planted in the right or the wrong spot!

Planning the garden for the first year is always a hassle. The task of trying to keep all the microclimates of the greenhouse in mind while selecting the various crops is further complicated when you attempt to satisfy the finicky needs of some vegetables and some vegetable eaters. Take it in easy steps, however, and the job will be done before you know it.

First, measure your garden and your greenhouse. Note which side faces south, and any shaded spots. Locate microclimates, and indicate which areas are bench or ground beds. If you have monitored your greenhouse, most of this information will be readily available, although, if it's your first year, there's very little chance that it was monitored. Special features that may be important for a crop—such as sun-lit water barrels or cosy brick or adobe heat-storage walls for heat-loving plants—should be drawn in.

Second, as you consider microclimates, local weather conditions, and inside and outside gardens, select the crops. Start record-keeping by noting, on the card for each type of crop, such information as soil type, light and space needs, temperature requirements, and conditions for successful germination.

Third, draw the garden to scale, large enough to read easily. Graph paper makes this task simple.

Fourth—and hardest—place each crop in its proper environment. All conditions important to good plant health must be considered. Such concerns as protection from insect pests, proper soil conditions, and temperature and light needs must be carefully orchestrated to produce a symphony of a vegetable garden.

To meet all (or most) of a plant's growth conditions does not necessarily require the abilities of a composer but it does need the skills of a juggler: juggle the cards that list the needs for each type of crop. Divide a sheet of paper into columns equal in number to the microclimates available in your green-house: full sun/hot; part shade/warm; part shade/cool, and so on. Then, using the cards, list each crop in all the micro-climates where it will grow. Next, juggle this information onto the large sheet of graph paper that is your garden. Locate each plant in its microclimate(s), tall plants to the back and short plants in the front. Shade-lovers can be tucked under tall plants, spiky plants can grow between foliage-producers, and plants that require little room can fit into small spaces next to large plants.

THE GREENHOUSE CROWD:
INTERPLANTING

The key to this kind of garden planning is called *interplanting,* or intercropping, an ancient technique of gardening with modern applications. The Indians always planted beans and squash in corn hills—on top of dead fish—because all these

plants fare better and produced more when grown together than when grown apart. Many primitive horticultural societies planted their gardens in clumps rather than in rows and interspersed plants that do not compete for the same environment—light, nutrients, moisture—within the same garden. Most greenhouse gardeners do too, for similar reasons. Several things are accomplished. First, plants may be grown closer together and still maintain optimal growth for each variety; non-competing plants are staggered, or zigzagged, for more effective use of space. Second, intercropping plants inhibits the easy transfer of disease or insects from plant to adjacent plant, because adjacent plants are different. This can mean the difference between losing one plant and losing an entire crop. In your greenhouse, interplanting can create a multi-season garden each year because as one crop finishes another takes its place. And, because the leaves of one plant may touch the leaves or stem of its neighbors, fewer weeds can take hold and less moisture evaporates from the soil. You get the same benefits as you do with a mulch.

In the limited space of the attached solar greenhouse it is impossible to provide red-carpet treatment for each plant, but each can have a close approximation by careful planning.

TIPS FOR INTERPLANTING

Rules for interplanting are simple and easy to follow.

1. You need a basic knowledge of the needs of each plant crop, so that no two crops that need the same things from the air or soil will be planted next to each other.

2. Do not plant two different root crops next to each other. They would use the same environment and attract the same root-attacking insects—although in the cool winter greenhouse, you can plant beets and turnips, both raised for greens, next to carrots if the first two are being raised for foliage and not for their fruit.

155

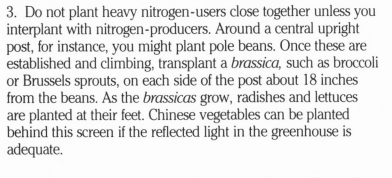

3. Do not plant heavy nitrogen-users close together unless you interplant with nitrogen-producers. Around a central upright post, for instance, you might plant pole beans. Once these are established and climbing, transplant a *brassica,* such as broccoli or Brussels sprouts, on each side of the post about 18 inches from the beans. As the *brassicas* grow, radishes and lettuces are planted at their feet. Chinese vegetables can be planted behind this screen if the reflected light in the greenhouse is adequate.

4. Do not plant tomatoes near nitrogen-producers. They will run to foliage rather than fruit if given too much of this nutrient.

5. Tall plants should not shade sun-loving plants or your heat storage. Tomatoes need the warmth and light found in the center of the cool winter greenhouse. A container of tomatoes suspended from the rafter takes advantage of a suitable micro-climate and does not cast shadows where they are not wanted.

6. Leeks and other members of the onion family grow nicely among low, foliage-producing plants.

7. Plants requiring maximum sun should be along the south edge of the bed, in the center of the bed, or in hanging baskets.

8. Herbs like the same conditions as tomatoes. If tomatoes grow in the ground-level bed, herbs can be grown just in front of them. Otherwise, make a hanging garden. (See June.)

9. Follow the suggestions listed in the companion planting chart. Many of these plants promote better health in each other as companions.

10. When a plant is beyond the stage of producing, pull it out and have another ready to take its place.

11. Because you are planting closely, you must stir the air in your greenhouse daily, either by venting on warm days or by using small fans on cool days.

GOOD FRIENDS:
COMPANION PLANTS

Companion plants are plants that in some way benefit each other. Basil, for instance, brings out the flavor of tomatoes and improves their growth patterns. Marigolds and nasturtiums are viewed as the primary companion plants of the outdoor organic garden, but the small greenhouse may not have room for them. I am so impressed with what they can do, however, that I put them in large containers—some hanging and others on the floor—so they can be located easily where they are needed. This way they take up little of the important growing area and are still around to help out. The one exception I make is to plant about four dwarf marigolds in my bed. These plants, which distract pests from nearby food plants, also repel nematodes in soil and must be in the bed to function.

Leeks, chives, radishes, lettuces and so on, lend themselves to intercropping and can become companion plants to most of the other greenhouse vegetables. They should be used liberally here and there in the garden and always planted in succession so that a crop is coming to maturity at all times.

Other than nasturtiums and marigolds, the plants listed here are common vegetables and herbs and are readily available through most seed companies. Two words of warning: Fennel seems to be disliked by most vegetables, so avoid planting it in your greenhouse. Cucumbers do not like strongly flavored herbs while the brassicas prefer them.

Companion planting may seem to be a juggling act at first, especially in conjunction with interplanting, but perseverance in learning to do it has immense rewards. Take advantage of the benefits of both.

S O M E   G O O D   F R I E N D S

	ROSEMARY	BASIL	BEANS, BUSH	BEANS, POLE	BRASSICAS	CARROTS	CUCUMBERS	SUMMER SAVORY	BEETS	EGGPLANT	LETTUCE	MARIGOLDS	NASTURTIUMS	GARLIC	CHIVES	LEEKS	PARSLEY	PEAS	PEPPERS	RADISHES	SAGE	SPINACH	STRAWBERRIES	TOMATOES	MELON	DILL	MINT
BEAN, POLE	✓					✓	✓	✓		✓	✓		✓							✓			✓	✓		✓	
BEAN, BUSH	✓				✓	✓	✓	✓	✓	✓	✓		✓							✓			✓	✓	✓	✓	
BEE BALM														✓										✓			
BEET			✓		✓																						
BORAGE														✓										✓	✓		
BRASSICAS	✓		✓									✓	✓								✓					✓	✓
CARROT	✓		✓	✓							✓				✓	✓	✓			✓	✓			✓			
CHAMOMILE					✓									✓													
CHIVES						✓																		✓			
CUCUMBER			✓	✓								✓	✓							✓	✓						
DILL				✓	✓									✓													
EGGPLANT			✓	✓																							
GARLIC	✓	✓						✓													✓					✓	✓
LEEK						✓																					
LEMON BALM														✓													
LETTUCE			✓	✓			✓																✓		✓		
MARJORAM														✓													
MELON			✓	✓								✓	✓							✓		✓					
MINT							✓							✓											✓		
PARSLEY														✓										✓			
PEA				✓				✓	✓												✓	✓				✓	
PEPPER			✓																						✓		
RADISH			✓	✓			✓						✓		✓										✓		
ROSEMARY			✓	✓	✓	✓								✓									✓				
SAGE	✓		✓	✓	✓	✓								✓						✓							
SPINACH																							✓				
STRAWBERRY			✓									✓	✓									✓					
SUMMER SAVORY			✓	✓										✓													
TARRAGON														✓													
THYME					✓									✓													
TOMATO		✓				✓						✓	✓	✓	✓		✓										✓

Table 8

CALENDARS

I've talked a lot about calendars and scheduling because planning is such an important part of raising vegetables or any other crop. Like record keeping, making up a calendar sounds like an unwelcome chore. The best way to start is to commandeer one of the new calendars that comes your way about this time of the year. If you have a choice, select the one with the most room for writing each day. However you do it, by November's end have the calendar for at least the first six months of next year ready and filled in. Some things—such as the time to transplant—depend upon conditions somewhat beyond your control, but you can list the dates for sowing, pruning, cleaning, taking cuttings, and so on, that do depend more on you.

Try not to make any block of time chock-full of things to do. Unplanned-for tasks always crop up. To allow for some of these, at least, I note when I can *expect to* transplant a crop, or repot a plant. This sets aside a specified amount of time for the task that I will get done sometime around the scheduled date, but maybe not on the exact day. And, of course, the calendar will change as time goes by. A spate of inclement weather may cause the fertilizing schedule to be revamped, or a change in vacation plans will result in a crop started later than originally planned. My usual problem is an over-full calendar from mid-May to mid-June, and a frenzy of work from September through October. I have not yet been able to schedule an easier work load at these times for myself, but scheduling does assure me that no job is forgotten.

Hang the calendar where it is highly visible. Both the current month and the next month hang above my work table to keep me aware of coming events. I've learned to check it first thing when I go out to the greenhouse. It is not enough to be aware of today's happenings. Look ahead for a few days so that what is done today doesn't have to be undone later. A copy of my calendar for last July appears here. Note the changes. I worked at our county fair and had to revamp the last part of July as a result, shifting planting and transplanting dates, feeding schedules, and so forth. By having everything on the calendar, I was fairly sure that none had been forgotten in the shuffle.

Calendars are also useful if you like to give plant gifts. You can allow enough time to grow the desired plant to its best stage to reflect the wish that goes with the gift. Miniature herb gardens can be vigorously healthy and present a nice aromatic tribute.

At the end of the year, save the calendars to help you plan the next year.

Calendar, garden plan, and seed catalogs at hand, you are now ready to begin turning dream into reality by writing an order for seeds.

JULY

SUNDAY	MONDAY	TUESDAY	WEDNESDAY	THURSDAY	FRIDAY	SATURDAY
DAILY: WATER ALL PLANTS WATER FLOORS 1-2 TIMES			SOW: EGGPLANT, ZUCCHINI, CUKES, W'MELON, BR. SPROUTS COLLARDS, BEANS, CELERY, CH. CABBAGE, PEPPERS, OKRA, LEEKS **1** DOMINION DAY (Canada)	**2** CLOUDY- NO WATER FEED	DIG UP, REWORK GROUND BED **3** CALL FOR MORE SAWDUST	**4** INDEPENDENCE DAY
5	TRANSPLANT TOMATOES **6** STARTED COMPOST PILE	**7**	**8** FEED	**9** TURNED COMPOST	**10**	**11**
12 TURNED COMPOST	**13** HOLIDAY (No Ireland)	SOW: BEETS, CARROTS, RUTABAGA **14** CLOUDY- NO WATER	**15** TURNED COMPOST FEED CLOUDY WATERED FLOOR	**16**	**17**	MAKE 4 BUSHELS 1-1-1 SOIL MIX **18** TURNED COMPOST
TRANSPLANT: BR. SPROUTS, BEANS, COLLARDS, PEPPERS, CH. CABBAGE. ZUCCHINI, CUKES, W'MELON TO LARGE CONTAINERS **19**	RENEW CAULK, PAINT IN 4 CUT **20** MOVE ALL PLANTS OUT	TO AUG **21** TURNED COMPOST	**22** FEED	**23**	TO AUG **24** TURNED COMPOST	MOVE PLANTS BACK IN **25** TRANSPLANT TOMATOES
SOW: COLLARDS, CH. CABBAGE, BEANS, ZUCCHINI, W'MELON, OKRA, EGGPLANT, PEAS, RADISHES **26**	**27** COMPOST SITS	**28**	TRANSPLANT BEETS RUTABAGAS TO GROUND BED **29** FEED TO AUG 3	**30** START COMPOST TO AUG 3 OR 4	**31**	

HOW TO ORDER SEEDS

Ordering seeds can be exasperating. Very few catalogs provide the information you need to calculate the number of plants you are going to grow from a packet of seeds and, when the information is provided, the percentage of seeds that will germinate is usually missing. However, by combining the information available in some of the seed catalogs I have worked out a method that is, for me, generally reliable.

If possible, obtain catalogs that do give the number of seeds in each packet. If you assume that 70 percent will germinate, you will have a *conservative* estimate of the number of plants you can raise from that packet. Most vegetable seed varieties will germinate at a rate of 80 percent, but some will germinate only 50 to 60 percent of the time. A few seed companies will actually tell you the number of plants to expect from one of their packets, a fairly reliable figure based on field tests. There is one catch: field tests are carried out using field growing techniques. The care the home gardener lavishes on his plants should increase this number. If you cannot obtain a catalog that gives the number of seeds per packet, the next best thing is to find one that gives instructions for *sowing* the crop. If you know how many seeds are planted to the inch or foot, and how many feet of row (or hills) the packet will plant, you can then figure out the approximate number of seeds it contains.

Some companies will tell you how many seeds are in an ounce. If their seed is sold in fractions of an ounce, simply divide the fraction into the number of seeds per ounce. Again, there is a catch: different varieties of the same crop have different-sized seeds. You take your chances.

Hybrid seeds, which tend to be more expensive than seeds of standard varieties, are often sold by count. You know exactly how many seeds you are buying. Unless the catalog also indicates the number of plants you can expect to grow from those seeds, you should still figure on a 70 percent germination rate.

A few companies offer small quantities of seeds for vegetables specifically adapted to greenhouse cultivation. While these seeds are expensive when purchased this way, the nature of the crop makes them surer bets for growing under glass. Seeds also are offered in a number of ways to make planting easier. Most have been developed for the commercial grower who sows seeds mechanically. *Pelletized* seeds are coated to make handling easier; most are small in size and difficult to sow thinly. The coating does not interfere with germination. Seeds are "glued" to *seed tapes* as they should be planted. All the gardener does is place the tape in a trench dug to the proper depth, and cover. *Sized* seeds, where the seeds are sized to pass through set openings in mechanical seeders, are sold primarily to farms and commercial growers.

The Dark of the Sun

DECEMBER

The climate:
cool to cold; the
shortest days of the year.
Some of the greenhouse takes
a rest although it remains
lush and green

The chores:
maintaining the cool garden;
starting new lettuce, in warmer
areas; harvesting tomatoes;
maintaining the cool garden and
protecting the status quo;
on the 21st: an eggnog to
celebrate the passing solstice
and the return of the sun

*D*ecember has Christmas. It also has the shortest day of the year—the winter solstice, the moment in the earth's annual cycle around the sun when its northern hemisphere reaches the limit of its tilt away from the sun and begins to swing back toward warmth again. This time, celebrated for some three weeks in ancient times, still has special meaning and special customs in many countries.

December is the month to look over our resources. Drop hints to Santa for greenhouse gardening books or, while the greenhouse is semi-dormant, take time to write for some of the information listed here. Every gardener is likely to feel the need to yell for help now and then.

Some plants take this time to go dormant. Even though they look green and perky, they may be napping. Growth has stopped. Dormancy can be caused by low light levels as well as low, or high, temperatures. Reduce water and food to dormant plants until they again show signs of life. And even though the garden has slowed, check it every day for bugs and problems. This takes very little time and lets you keep in touch with the plants.

December, finally, is the month when you may harvest those lovely tomatoes started last July. You no longer have to imagine the taste. Sample one, and let the juice dribble down your chin.

HELP

Growing food in a solar greenhouse is an exciting venture. It also can be frustrating. There are few places you can go when you need information or assistance with a problem. This chapter may answer some of your cries for help. In it you will find general information, lists of magazines and organizations specializing in food production under glass, purveyors of seeds and horticultural supplies, books, people, and whatever else I have found to give me information I needed. No prices are noted because they probably will have changed at least twice before you will read this.

Solar Greenhouse Design

McCullagh, James C., Ed., *The Solar Greenhouse Book,* Rodale Press, Emmaus, Pa. 18049 (1978). A source of good information on the design, construction, and use of solar greenhouses. Has many useful charts.

Yanda, Bill, and Rick Fisher, *The Food and Heat Producing Solar Greenhouse: Design, Construction, and Operation,* John Muir Press, Santa Fe, N.M. 87501 (1976; revised second edition 1980). The bible of do-it-yourself solar greenhouse design and construction.

General Information and Periodicals

Bailey, Liberty H., *The Standard Cyclopedia of Horticulture* (3 vols.), New York: The Macmillan Co. (1928). If you can find a copy of this work, you are indeed fortunate. It covers the practices of culture for all plants useful to man that were sold then by seed companies, nurserymen, and others dealing in plants. It also covers diseases and pests, botanical information, and much more. Some of this information is no longer available in modern books on gardening.

Bailey, Liberty H., *The Standard Cyclopedia of Horticulture* (3 vols.), New York: The Macmillan Co. (1942). Not a rewrite of Bailey's earlier *Cyclopedia*. These books are broader in scope, and cover many of the new varieties introduced in the 1930s and 1940s. It also includes plant varieties offered for sale by European seed and plant dealers in North America, and tropical plants found in U.S. possessions abroad. This work discusses the cultivation of many plants no longer extensively found in American gardens, and is essential to those gardeners interested in regenerating interest in these varieties.

Bailey, Liberty H., *Manual of Gardening: A Practical Guide*, New York: The Macmillan Co. (1930). Cultivation of flowers, fruits, and vegetables for the home gardener. Much of this information should be of interest to greenhouse growers.

DeKorne, James B., *The Survival Greenhouse*, The Walden Foundation, P.O. Box 5, El Rito, N.M. 87530 (1975). A case study of food production in a small greenhouse, with hydroponics, aquaculture, rabbits, and earthworms. Lots of practical information.

New England Solar Energy Association (NESEA), *Proceedings of the Marlboro College Conference on Energy Conserving Solar Heated Greenhouses* (1977), and, with the Alternative Energy Institute, *Proceedings of the Second National Conference on Energy Conserving Solar Greenhouses* (1979). Both can be obtained from NESEA, Brattleboro, Vt., 05301. Excellent practical experience from those who have been operating solar greenhouses.

American Horticulturist and *News and Views*, American Horticultural Society, Mount Vernon, Va., 22121; for the advanced gardener.

The Family Food Garden, The Webb Company, 1999 Shepherd Rd., St. Paul, Minn. 55116. Backyard food production and gardening under glass.

The Planter, Hobby Greenhouse Association, P.O. Box 951, Wallingford, Conn. 06492. This organization also offers information services, consulting, and answers to inquiries, that are worth the price of the subscription many times over.

Plants Alive Magazine, 2603 Third Ave., Seattle, Wash. 98121 is dedicated to the art of growing all sorts of plants in containers and under glass.

Organic Gardening, Rodale Press, Inc., 33 E. Minor St., Emmaus, Pa. 18049, is a practical source on all types of food production in the home garden, greenhouse, and small farm.

Solar Living and Solar Greenhouse Digest, P.O. Box 2626, Flagstaff, Ariz. 86033 concentrates on growing plants in the solar greenhouse. Many articles by those who have learned the necessary techniques.

People and Organizations

American Horticultural Society, Mount Vernon, Va 22121. Two bimonthly periodicals on growing plants outside and indoors for the advanced growers.

Amity Foundation, 2760 Riverview, Eugene, Ore. 97403. Runs a demonstration aquaculture/agriculture system in a solar greenhouse. Tours of the facility, workshops, and information.

Department of Horticulture, Ohio Agricultural Research & Development Center, Wooster, Ohio 44691. A large experimental greenhouse program including the use of waste heat and testing of vegetable crops. Many publications.

Berkshire Garden Center, Education Office, Stockbridge, Mass. 01262. Intensive crop production in a solar greenhouse. Demonstrations and information.

Center for Local Self-Reliance, 3302 Chicago Ave., Minneapolis, Minn. 55407. Lectures and slide shows on solar greenhouse management.

Clivus Multrum, Inc., 14-A Eliot St., Cambridge, Mass. 02138. Abby Rockefeller and Carl Lindstrom have experimented with the use of grey-water systems in solar greenhouses. Some publications.

Coolidge Center for the Advancement of Agriculture, River Hill Farm, Topsfield, Mass. 01983. A demonstration farm featuring low–cost, solar greenhouses for small farms and suburban dwellers. Some publications and information.

Integral Urban House, Farallones Institute, 1516 Fifth St., Berkeley, Cal. 94710. Workshops and information on biological solar greenhouse management, aquaculture, and other low energy technologies.

The Herb Society of America, 300 Huntington Ave., Boston, Mass. 02115. Has periodicals, publications, and a library on growing herbs.

Hobby Greenhouse Association, P.O. Box 951, Wallingford, Conn. 06492. Offers information, library services, and a monthly periodical on greenhouse growing.

Barrett Hill Farm, Wilton, N.H. 03086, has workshops on food self-sufficiency, including food production under glass.

New Alchemy Institute, P.O. Box 432, Woods Hole, Mass. 02543 has been experimenting with biological management of integrated solar greenhouses, including aquaculture, small scale intensive agriculture, and the greenhouse environment. Workshops, tours, and publications are available.

Solar Survival, Cherry Hill, Harrisville, N.H. 03450, specializes in food self-sufficiency and winter gardening techniques.

Solar Sustenance Team, Rt. 1, Box 107 AA, Santa Fe, N.M. 87501, sponsors workshops on biological solar greenhouse management. Information and slide shows available.

Tilth, Rt. 2, Box 190-A, Arlington, Wash. 98223, is an organization of West Coast organic gardeners and solar greenhouse growers. Publications are available.

Greenhouse Supplies

Equipment for the residential greenhouse is difficult to obtain. Most suppliers cater strictly to commercial growers. The following should help:

A. M. Leonard, Inc., 6665 Spiker Rd., Piqua, Ohio 54356. Horticultural supplies by mail for the residential grower. Free catalog.

Seeds and Plants

I, or my friends, have used many of these seed sources. Inclusion of seed companies in this listing does *not* constitute an endorsement of their products. Variables, such as climate, greenhouse design, and gardening techniques will cause differences in crop performance and yield. Select companies that produce seeds in environments similar to your greenhouse.

Oriental Vegetables:

Chientan & Co., 1001 S. Alvarado St., Los Angeles, Cal. 90006

Herbst Bros. Seedsmen, Inc., 100 N. Main St., Brewster, N.Y. 10509

J. L. Hudson, P.O. Box 1058, Redwood City, Cal. 94064

Kitasawa, 356 W. Taylor, San Jose, Cal. 94002

R. H. Shumway, Rockford, Ill. 61101

Stokes Seeds, Box 548, Buffalo, N.Y. 14240

Tsang & Ma International, P.O. Box 294, Belmont, Cal. 94002

Herbs:

Calumet Herb Co., P.O. Box 248, South Holland, Ill. 60473

Chientan & Co., 1001 S. Alvarado St., Los Angeles, Cal. 90006

Comstock, Ferre & Co., Wethersfield, Conn. 06109

Hilltop Herb Co., P.O. Box 866, Cleveland, Tex. 77327

Jardin du Gourmet, West Danville, Vt. 05873

Nichol's Garden Nursery, 1190 N. Pacific Highway, Albany, Ore. 97321

Pine Hill Farms, P.O. Box 144, Rosewell, Ga., 30075

Seed Companies:

Abundant Life Seed Foundation, P.O. Box 374, Gardiner, Wash. 98334. Winter-hardy and hard to find varieties. Catalog $1.

J.A. Demonchaux Co., 827 N. Kansas Ave., Topeka, Kans. 66608. U.S. outlet for the great French seedhouse Vilmourin-Andrieux. Many winter-hardy seeds and European varieties. Great catalog.

Farmer Seed and Nursery Co., Faribault, Minn. 55021. Excellent source of seeds for the Northern Great Plains and Great Lakes Area.

Graham Center Seed Directory, Rt. 3, Box 95, Wadesboro, N.C. 28170. Lists small seed companies carrying traditional seed varieties.

Joseph Harris Co., Inc., Moreton Farm, Rochester, N.Y. 14624. Harris seeds do very well in the adverse conditions of the New England summer and elsewhere. Very reliable.

Herbst Bros. Seedsmen, Inc. 100 N. Main St., Brewster, N.Y. 10509. They carry a line of cold-hardy plants as well as regular garden crops.

Nichol's Garden Nursery, 1190 N. Pacific Highway, Albany, Ore. 97321. Nichol's carries varieties adapted to the Northwest. They also do well in the Northeast.

Johnny's Select Seeds, Albion, Maine 04910. Crops adapted to the northern states and the greenhouse. Catalog is a book on horticulture in itself.

Park's Seed Co., Greenwood, S.C. 29647. An excellent source of seeds for the warm weather greenhouse and southern growers.

Stoke's Seeds, Inc., Buffalo, N.Y. 14240. Offers more plant varieties than any other seed company: cold-hardy, heat-tolerant, and greenhouse specialties. Excellent growing information.

Thompson & Morgan, Box 100, Farmingdale, N.J. 07727. An outlet of a famous English seed company. Some winter-hardy crops and continental favorites.

Advanced Vegetable Gardening

Jeavons, John, *How to Grow More Vegetables Than You Ever Thought Possible on Less Land Than You Can Imagine,* Ecology Action of the Midpeninsula, 2225 El Camino Real, Palo

Alto, Cal. 94306 (1974). A Biodynamic/French Intensive method of gardening described step-by-step. Can be successfully applied to greenhouse production for increased yields.

U.S. Department of Agriculture, *Growing Vegetables in the Home Garden*, Home and Garden Bulletin No. 202. Single copies free from your congressman. Charts on planting quantities with expected yield, last spring and first fall frost dates, and much other information also applicable to the greenhouse.

Saving Seed

Hills, Lawrence D., *Save Your Own Seed*, The Henry Doubleday Research Association, Bocking, Braintree, Essex, England. An informative book on practical home methods of saving all sorts of seeds.

True Seed Exchange, Kent Whaley, RR 1, Princeton, Mo. 64673. An organization of serious gardeners interested in preserving heirloom vegetable varieties in danger of extinction. They also experiment with crops and report their results in a monthly newsletter. Members trade or sell seeds to each other. The membership fee includes a membership list, companion planting chart, newsletter and *Seed Saving Guide*.

Fruits

These books were excellent guides in setting up our home orchard and starting us on the road to greenhouse fruit growing.

Hill, Lewis, *Fruits and Berries for the Home Garden*, New York: Alfred A. Knopf (1977). Broad coverage of the fruits grown in small gardens and orchards. Includes the varieties best grown in various climates, how to propagate them, plant, grow, and harvest them. Information on pruning each fruit and on the diseases most likely to attack.

Kraft, Ken and Pat, *Grow Your Own Dwarf Fruit Trees,* New York: Walker and Co. (1974). Specifically describes the varieties of dwarf fruit trees available, and details the cultivation of each. Pruning techniques are illustrated. Sources for each variety are given.

Simmons, Alan, *Potted Orchards,* London: David and Charles (1975). One of the nicest references for orchards grown in glass houses, this work gives full details on fruit cultivation.

Simmons, Alan, *Growing Unusual Fruit,* New York: Walker and Co. (1972). This book and the following one introduce the art of growing fruit under glass. Provides the basic details necessary to cultivate each fruit and lists varieties suited to the climate where the fruit grows best, this includes fruit not traditionally grown in greenhouses.

Southwick, Lawrence, *Dwarf Fruit Trees for the Home Gardener,* Charlotte, Vt: Garden Way Publishing Co. (1972). An excellent little book on the design and care of the small home dwarf fruit orchard. The methods are not always organic, but coverage of the subject is quite complete and useful to the greenhouse orchardist. Pruning and cultivation methods, in many instances, can be carried into the greenhouse.

As for the old masters, try to find books written by Thomas Rivers, an English nurseryman, or Liberty H. Bailey.

Soils

US Department of Agriculture, *Soil: Yearbook of Agriculture,* Washington, DC: Government Printing Office (1957), or a second-hand book store. Complete coverage of soils and their effects on plant growth. More technical than Maddox, but a more complete coverage of U.S. soils. Both organic and chemical soil treatment methods offered.

Maddox, Harry, *Your Garden Soil,* North Pomfret, Vt: David and Charles, Inc. (1974). A synthesis of plant soil science and centuries of accumulated gardening lore into a practical handbook on garden soils and their effects on plant growth.

Staff of Organic Gardening and Farming, eds., *Organic Fertilizers: Which Ones and How to Use Them,* Emmaus, Pa: Rodale Press, Inc. (1973). This book wraps up all you need to know about the subject. It is very handy for the organic gardener because it tells how much to use of each and explains what they do in the soil and for plant growth.

Pests and Diseases

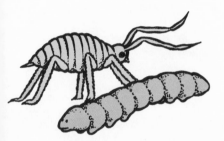

US Department of Agriculture, *Plant Diseases; Yearbook of Agriculture,* Washington, DC: Government Printing Office (1953), or a second-hand book store. An excellent coverage of plant diseases. Controls vary from organic to chemical. Knowing the behavior, or life cycle, of the disease helps the organic gardener in disease control.

Agricultural Research Service, USDA, Beltsville Agricultural Research Center, Rm. 251, Bldg. 003, Beltsville, Md. 20705. Publications and information on garden pests and biological controls.

Editors of Organic Gardening Magazine, *The Organic Way to Plant Protection,* Emmaus, Pa: Rodale Press, Inc. (1966). Discusses each crop, its disease and pest problems, and their cures or controls.

Rincon-Vitova Insectaries, Inc., P.O. Box 95, Oak Vino, Cal. 93022. Carries most beneficial insects including *Encarsia formosa* and Ladybugs.

Gothard, Inc., P.O. Box 367, Canutillo, Tex. Carries the *Trichogramma* wasp and Praying Mantis egg cases.

Better Yield Insects, 13310 Riverside Drive East, Tecumseh, Ont. N8N 1B2, Canada, has *Encarsia formosa* at good prices. To import them into this country, apply for a *free* permit from: USDA Permit Unit, Rm 635 Federal Building, Hyattsville, Md. 20782. This permit must be sent with your order.

Greenhouse Environment

Mastalerz, John W., *The Greenhouse Environment,* New York: John Wiley & Sons (1977). Technical treatise of the effects of environment on plant growth. Most informative; for the advanced grower.

Beckford, Elwood D., and Stuart Dunn, *Lighting for Plant Growth,* Kent, Ohio: Kent State University Press (1972). Study of the effects of light on plant growth.

Canham, A. E., *Artificial Light in Horticulture,* Eindhoven, Netherlands: Centrix Publishing Co. (1966). Discusses the light needs of various food crops and ways to augment low light levels. Technical but understandable. This should be available at most state universities offering courses on horticulture.

Lawrence, W. J. C., *Science in the Glasshouse,* Edinburgh: Oliver & Boyd (1963). Discusses the light requirements of plants grown in glass houses in Europe. Technical, but not beyond the amateur gardener.

Weather

National Climatic Center, Federal Building, Asheville, N.C. 28801. Repository of our national weather data. Write, requesting full detailed weather for your locality by naming nearest large city or airport. There is a fee for this service.

Climates of the States (2 vols.), and *Weather Atlas of the United States,* Gale Research Co., Book Tower, Detroit, Mich. 48226. Contains detailed weather information organized by reporting

weather station. Not all stations are included, but representative sampling gives general weather patterns.

US Department of Agriculture, *Climate and Man: Yearbook of 1941,* reprinted by Gale Research Co., Detroit, Mich. You might look for this in a second-hand book store also. It ties climate and agricultural practices into a neat bundle that has not gone out-of-date.

Aquaculture in the Greenhouse

Bardach, John, John Ryther, and William McLarney, *Aquaculture: The Farming and Husbandry of Freshwater and Marine Organisms,* Somerset, N.J.: John Wiley & Sons, (1972). The most important work on the subject. McLarney has worked on aquaculture projects for New Alchemy Institute for a number of years.

Head, William, and Jon Splane, *Fish Farming in Your Solar Greenhouse,* Eugene, Ore. 97403. Amity Foundation. For the beginner on a small scale.

Straw Bale Horticulture

Allen, P.G., "Growing Glasshouse Crops in Straw: A Survey of Recent Developments", in *National Agricultural Advisory Service Quarterly Review,* vol. 80, pages 167–174, 1968. Look for this in your state university or horticultural society library. An interesting technique.

Laughton, A., "Straw-bale Culture of Greenhouse Crops", in the *Proceedings of the International Symposium on Controlled Environment Agriculture,* Tucson, Arix. (1977), pages 208–215.

APPENDIX

C limate is the single most important element in determining how you deal with a solar greenhouse, what you grow there and when you grow it. Solar greenhouses respond to outside conditions of weather. Unlike conventional greenhouses, they depend on guile and knowledge to get them through cold dark seasons, not the brute force of fossil fueled heaters. Therefore, every solar greenhouse is different from every other solar greenhouse, and the greenhouse gardener needs to know both climate—the general state of things in a particular area—and weather, the particular set of hot and cold running conditions outside at any given moment.

The weather is of interest to us all. A comment on the present state of the weather follows "how do you do?" and can always be relied upon as a topic of conversation when all else fails. Cloudy days, rain, or a heat spell can make us feel out of sorts, in the dumps; the sun, on the other hand, makes us happy, gives us pep, lightens our steps. Plants respond in much the same way. In a solar greenhouse, the colder the temperature, the more energy must be supplied or trapped inside to maintain a climate in which plants can grow. Wind plays its part in this scheme of things, entering through all sorts of cracks and crevices to play havoc with stored heat and temperatures. I had one spot in my greenhouse that would freeze every winter night that we had strong wind. I finally had to light a candle one stormy night, to trace the icy blast to its source—a pinhole leak in the caulk between two panes of glass.

Even more important than temperature (crops can grow in a rather broad range of temperature) is the amount of sunlight available to them, and the form in which that sunlight reaches them. As direct radiation, sunlight provides bright light and lots of warmth. Diffuse sunlight may provide light nearly as bright, but not much heat—and this may make the difference between a cool or a warm winter greenhouse garden. Light is diffused by air pollution, by the angle at which the sun's rays hit the earth or the glass of the greenhouse, and by such weather phenomena as clouds or ice particles suspended in the atmosphere. It can be scattered by snow-covered ground, concrete paving, or nearby reflectors (such as glass windows in neighboring houses). Hours of daylight, the total length of time between sunrise and sunset, combine with percentages of direct or diffuse radiation to affect light supply. The gardener should be aware of all of them.

To help, by supplying information not widely and easily available, these monthly climate maps detail *general* weather conditions for the U.S. It may not describe your specific climate very accurately, so if you need more detailed information, write the National Weather Center, Federal Building, Asheville, N.C., 28801, including the name of your nearest weather station, large city, or major airport. There is a small charge for this service.

The data here come from three sources. Map and temperature isobars (lines connecting points of like temperature) are taken from *The Climatic Atlas of the U.S.* (1967). The monthly hours of daylight are listed in the *Smithsonian Meteorological Tables* (Sixth Edition). The percentages of those hours likely to be sunny are taken from *The Climates of the States* (1974). Climate data represent averages taken over a thirty-year period to establish norms. Those norms are revised every ten years, to identify trends.

HOW TO USE THE MAPS

Temperature: Your average daily temperature for the month will be somewhere between the isobars on either side of your location. It can be guestimated by how close you are to one or the other isobar. The average daily temperature can also give you average night and average day temperatures, as follows: for night temperatures, subtract 10° to 15°F from the average; for day temperatures, add 10° to 15°F. Remember that these are averages and that actual temperatures (particularly at the beginnings and ends of months) will vary.

Hours of daylight: The length of a day depends on the height of the sun in the sky, which is a factor of latitude—those arcing lines that go from one side of the map to the other. Read the daily average number of hours of sun for the month, for the latitudes on each side of your location, from the figures on the right side of the map, then extrapolate them for your latitude.

Notice that there is not much seasonal change in day length in southern areas—but as you near the 48 degrees of latitude the difference is substantial. In summer, day length is longer in the north than in the south. Long days, even if sunlight is diffused, is important to many plants because it triggers fruit production.

The amount of sunlight that will be direct radiation unhindered by clouds or fog is shown by the colors of the maps. A key to the colors on the bottom of each page will translate them into percentages of daylight hours. Again, these are averages that may not describe your particular patch of earth accurately. Assess local conditions—haziness, cloud cover, air pollution, as you decide whether there is enough light for growth.

Flipping through the twelve maps for the months of the year can give you a quick idea of the patterns of weather for your particular location. Such features as large bodies of water, mountains, or plains can affect them greatly. So can small geographical features, hills, streams, even highways. Weather does not perform to artificial boundaries. Note, and plan accordingly.

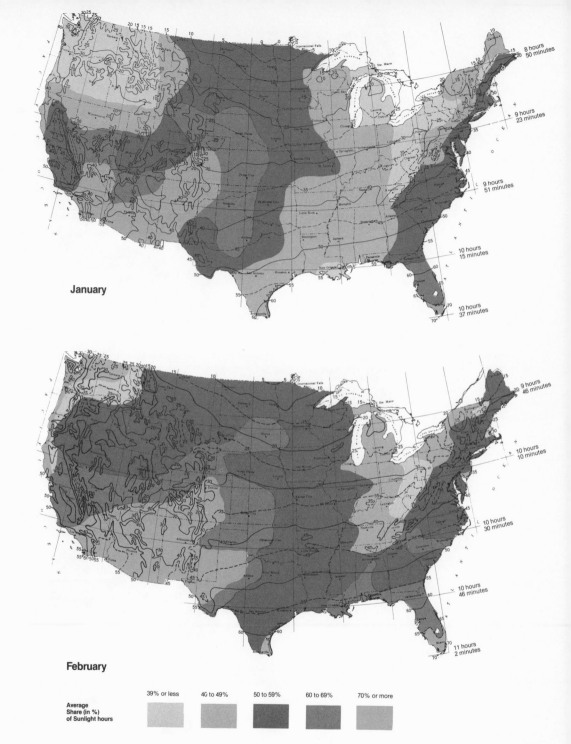

January

8 hours
50 minutes

9 hours
23 minutes

9 hours
51 minutes

10 hours
15 minutes

10 hours
37 minutes

9 hours
46 minutes

10 hours
10 minutes

10 hours
30 minutes

10 hours
46 minutes

11 hours
2 minutes

February

Average Share (in %) of Sunlight hours	39% or less	40 to 49%	50 to 59%	60 to 69%	70% or more

181

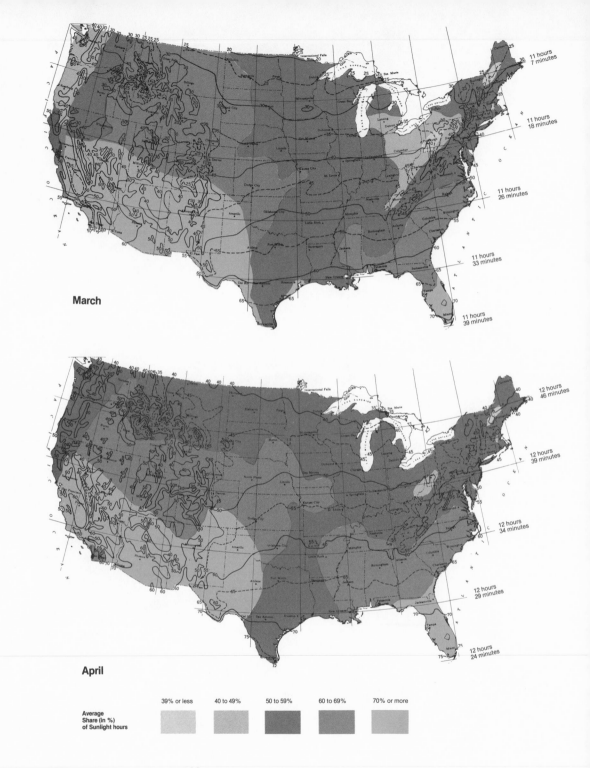

March

11 hours
7 minutes

11 hours
18 minutes

11 hours
26 minutes

11 hours
33 minutes

11 hours
39 minutes

April

12 hours
46 minutes

12 hours
39 minutes

12 hours
34 minutes

12 hours
29 minutes

12 hours
24 minutes

Average Share (in %) of Sunlight hours	39% or less	40 to 49%	50 to 59%	60 to 69%	70% or more

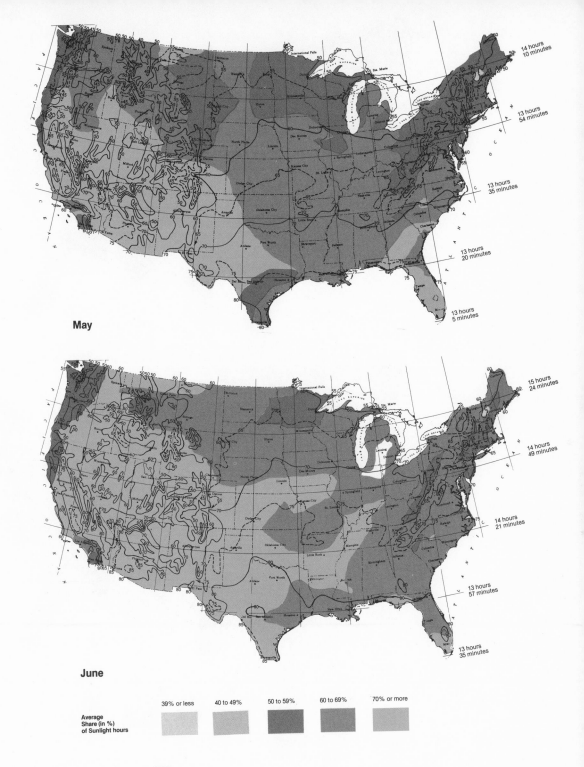

May

June

14 hours
10 minutes

13 hours
54 minutes

13 hours
35 minutes

13 hours
20 minutes

13 hours
5 minutes

15 hours
24 minutes

14 hours
49 minutes

14 hours
21 minutes

13 hours
57 minutes

13 hours
35 minutes

Average
Share (in %)
of Sunlight hours

| 39% or less | 40 to 49% | 50 to 59% | 60 to 69% | 70% or more |

183

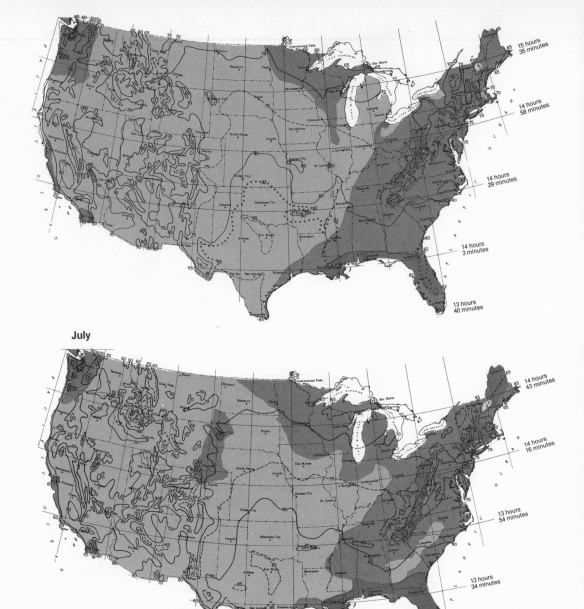

July

August

Average
Share (in %)
of Sunlight hours

39% or less	40 to 49%	50 to 59%	60 to 69%	70% or more

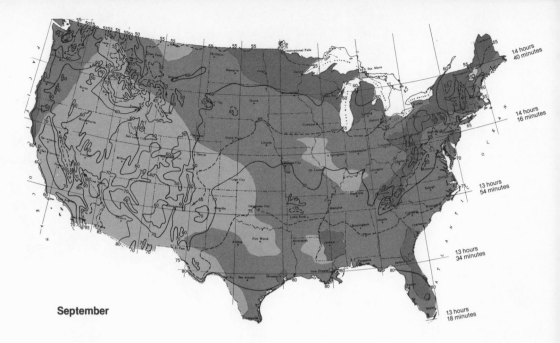

14 hours
40 minutes

14 hours
16 minutes

13 hours
54 minutes

13 hours
34 minutes

13 hours
18 minutes

September

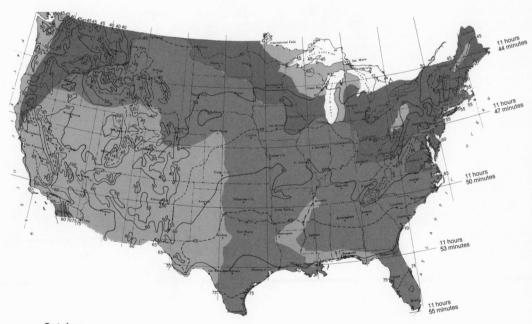

11 hours
44 minutes

11 hours
47 minutes

11 hours
50 minutes

11 hours
53 minutes

11 hours
55 minutes

October

Average Share (in %) of Sunlight hours	39% or less	40 to 49%	50 to 59%	60 to 69%	70% or more

185

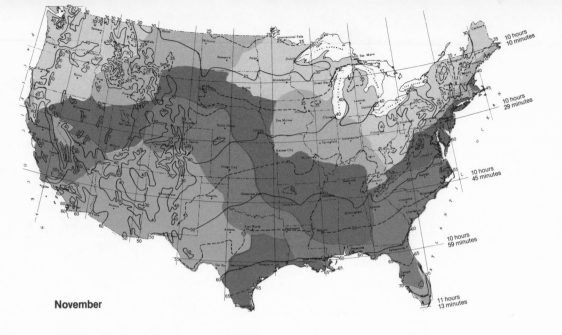

10 hours
10 minutes

10 hours
29 minutes

10 hours
45 minutes

10 hours
59 minutes

11 hours
13 minutes

November

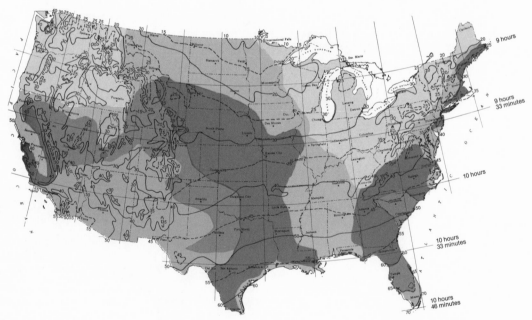

9 hours

9 hours
33 minutes

10 hours

10 hours
33 minutes

10 hours
46 minutes

December

Average
Share (in %)
of Sunlight hours

39% or less   40 to 49%   50 to 59%   60 to 69%   70% or more

186

THE BEAUFORT WIND SCALE

The Beaufort Wind Scale may be used to estimate wind speeds near the greenhouse. Wind speed data should be recorded on the chart illustrated on page 24. Wind, passing across the south-facing greenhouse glass, may directly influence interior temperatures.

Beaufort Number	General Description	Look for	Wind velocity (miles per hour)
		THE BEAUFORT SCALE	
0	Calm	Smoke rises vertically, no air movement.	Less than 1
1	Light air	Smoke drifts; weather vanes do not move.	1 to 3
2	Light breeze	Weather vanes move; air movement felt on the face; leaves rustle.	4 to 7
3	Gentle breeze	Leaves and small twigs in constant motion; small flags extended.	8 to 12
4	Moderate breeze	Moves small branches; moves dust and loose paper.	13 to 18
5	Fresh breeze	Small leafy trees sway; whitewater on inland waterways.	19 to 24
6	Strong breeze	Large branches move; electric and telephone wires whistle.	25 to 31
7	Moderate gale	Whole trees in motion; difficult to walk against wind.	32 to 48
8	Fresh gale	Twigs snap off trees; hard to walk	39 to 46
9	Strong gale	Removes loose roof coverings; may do some minor structural damage.	47 to 54
10	Full gale	Generally along coast; uproots trees; major structural damage possible.	55 to 63
11	Storm	Widespread damage.	64 to 72
12 and up	Hurricane	Widespread damage.	73 and up

The Beaufort Scale was devised in 1806 by Admiral Sir E. Beaufort, based on the effect of wind on a fullrigged man-of-war of that era. In 1874, the International Meteorological Committee adapted the scale for international weather use. In 1912, wind speeds were allocated to the Beaufort Numbers after standards for measurement were established. This chart uses the descriptions and numbers established in 1946 by the International Meteorological Committee.

187

Index

onion family, 2, 15, 17, 53, 107, 109, 112
oranges, 61-63
organic fertilizers, 41, 44-51
Oriental vegetables, 13, 14, 17, 109, 112

P

parsnips, 109
pasteurization, soils, 41
peaches, 69-70
pears, 70
peas, 13, 15, 17, 29, 109, 112
peppers, 29, 53, 81
pests and diseases, 123-139
    (see also specific bug or disease)
    biological controls, 175-176
pH, 40
phosphorus, 42
pill bugs, 133
planning, 152-162
plant bugs, 134
plums, 70
potassium, 42-43
propagation, asexual, 61-62, 84-88
    cuttings, 86-87
    division, 87
    equipment, 84-85
    grafting, 62
    layering, 61-62
    propagation beds and boxes, 85-86
    soils, 84
propagation, sexual, 31-39, 83

Q

quarantine, 115, 128

selection, 32, 34-35, 102, 118, 161-162
sowing, 34
viability, 119-120

R

rabbits, 11-12
radishes, 110, 112
records, 141-147, 153-154, 159-160
    and saving seeds, 117
    microclimates, 19-24, 146
rhubarb, 69
    poisonous leaves, 69
roots, cold, 4-6
    nutrient transport, 4, 6
rutabagas (see turnips)

S

scale insects, 135
seedlings, summer garden, 32-39, 52-53
seedlings, winter gardens, 103-104, 105-112
seeds
    catalogs, 152, 161-162
    germination percentage, 120, 161-162
    ordering, 152, 161-162
    preservation, 120-121
    saving, 115-121
seeds, saving, 117-120
slugs and snails, 46, 135
soil, 4-5, 35-37, 39-44, 46, 98-99, 103, 135
    basic greenhouse, 40
sowbugs, 133
spider mites, 133-134
spinach, 16-17, 29, 110, 112
squash, 29, 53

strawberries, 59-61
sunshine, hours of, 11
   maps, 181-187
   percent possible, 11, 22
sweet potatoes, 34, 53

T

temperature, 4-6, 21, 24
   average daily, 11, 181-187
thrips, 136
Tobacco Mosaic Virus, 138
tomatoes, 29, 53, 100-102
transplanting, 37
True Seed Exchange, 118
turnip greens, 15, 17, 110, 112

V

vegetables, warm weather garden, 74-76
ventilation, 7
viticulture, 65-66

W

warm weather garden, 73-77, 80-81, 83, 89-95
water, 8-9
watering schedule, 9
weather, 10-11
   Beaufort Wind Scale, 24, 187
   maps, 181-186
   National Weather Center, 11, 176
weevils, 136
whitefly, 136-137
wilts, 139
winter garden, 97-100, 102-112

THE TEXT OF THIS BOOK WAS SET IN 12
POINT CHELTENHAM BOOK, A NEW CUT
BY COMPUGRAPHIC OF A DISTINGUISHED
OLD FACE. THE TYPE IS LEADED ONE POINT.

THIS BOOK WAS DESIGNED BY MICHAEL
HAVEY AND PRODUCED BY PAULA KURSH.
ALL COMPOSITION IS BY JOANIE AND CAROL,
AT WINZELER TYPOGRAPHY, MANCHESTER,
NEW HAMPSHIRE.